Authorisms

Authorisms

Words Wrought by Writers

PAUL DICKSON

BLOOMSBURY

NEW YORK · LONDON · NEW DELHI · SYDNEY

Published by Bloomsbury USA, New York

Bloomsbury is a trademark of Bloomsbury Publishing Plc

All papers used by Bloomsbury USA are natural, recyclable products made
from wood grown in well-managed forests. The manufacturing processes
conform to the environmental regulations of the country of origin.

LIBRARY OF CONGRESS CATALOGING-IN-PUBLICATION DATA

Dickson, Paul.
Authorisms: Words Wrought by Writers /
Paul Dickson.—First U.S. Edition.
pages cm
Includes bibliographical references and index.
ISBN 978-1-62040-540-6 (hardback)
1. Literature—Philosophy. 2. Lexicography in literature. 3. Influence
(Literary, artistic, etc.) 4. Linguistics in literature. I. Title.
PN54.D53 2014
801'.3—dc23
2013038417

First U.S. Edition 2014

1 3 5 7 9 10 8 6 4 2

Typeset by Hewer Text UK Ltd, Edinburgh

Printed and bound in the U.S.A. by Thomson-Shore, Inc., Dexter, Michigan

Bloomsbury books may be purchased for business or promotional use.
For information on bulk purchases please contact Macmillan Corporate
and Premium Sales Department at specialmarkets@macmillan.com.

To two fellow writers who have helped me from the start: Joseph C. Goulden, good friend and fellow author who has helped me with all of my books beginning with my first, *Think Tanks*, published in 1971, and to Robert Skole, good friend, former boss, collaborator, and idea man extraordinaire. Thanks, Joe and Bob.

Published April 23, 2014, in honor of that day in 1564 marking the sesquiquadricentennial, or 450th anniversary of the birth of William Shakespeare, now and forever the greatest neologist of the English language.*

---

* The term *sesquiquadricentennial* was coined by John M. Morse and the staff of Merriam-Webster for the purposes of this work.

A man in all the world's new fashion planted,
That hath a mint of phrases in his brain

—Shakespeare, *All's Well That Ends Well*

Making up words is a respectable business, occasionally
blessed with wide acceptance. Whoever made up innies and
outies to describe navels that are either recessed or protruding
must have experienced some satisfaction.

—Dave Matheny, *Star Tribune*,
Newspaper of the Twin Cities, November 6, 1988

Contents

AU´THOR`ISM ą´thĕr`ĭz'm n. [from Middle English auctour, from Anglo-French auctor, autor, from Latin auctor promoter, originator, author, from augēre to increase + -nym "name"] 1. Obs. Authorship; the position or character of an author. From the letters of Horace Walpole (V.3): "a sensible man, but has not worn off his authorism yet, and thinks there is nothing so charming as writers, and to be one." 2. The irresistible impulse for one to become an author in one form or another. This impulse often affects even those who have no right being an author. (*Urban Dictionary*) 3. Word, phrase or name created by or an existing term given a new meaning by an author or journalist; a literary neologism. William Shakespeare whose written vocabulary consisted of 17, 245 words including hundreds of authorisms. Some of them, true nonce words, never went further than their appearance in his plays, but others—like *bump*, *hurry*, *critical*, and *road*—are essential parts of our standard vocabulary today.

INTRODUCTION

The Sweet Click

Writers have long enjoyed their ability to create new words, to neologize—to write, read, and hear—what writer Arthur Plotnik, who has written on the subject of neologism in literature, calls the "sweet click of coinage" and which he terms one of the rewards of the vocation.

Early writers got to hear a lot of those clicks as they helped shape the language, beginning with **Geoffrey Chaucer**, who had a field day being the one to first leave a written record of several thousand words. The many words regarded as his coinages include *bed, bagpipe, Martian,* and *universe.* **Sir Thomas More**, who died in 1535, gets credit for having invented or discovered among many others—*anticipate, explain,* and *fact.*[1] **John Milton**, who died in 1674, as far as can be determined minted such terms as *impassive, earthshaking, lovelorn,* and *by hook or crook.* He also coined the expression *all hell broke loose.*

"Milton," wrote critic, essayist, and Milton scholar Logan Pearsall Smith in his *Milton and His Modern Critics*, "felt himself perfectly at liberty to lay tribute on all the possible resources of the nation's linguistic coffers, from old archaic words to the new words he created for himself out of the rags and fragments found in their recesses. For Milton often coined the words he wanted, and the *Oxford Dictionary* finds in his writings the first appearance of many words which are now familiar to us all. They may possibly have been used before, yet, like the coins of a great king, they seem to bear his image stamped upon them."

Smith then listed his own favorite Miltonisms: *dimensionless, infinitude, emblazonry, liturgical, bannered, ensanguined, horrent, anarchy, Satanic, echoing, irradiance,* and his great chaotic word *pandemonium*.[2] According to Gavin Alexander, lecturer in English at Cambridge and fellow of Milton's alma mater, Christ's College, who has mined the *Oxford English Dictionary* (*OED*) for evidence, Milton is responsible for introducing some 630 words to the English language, making him that country's greatest neologist. As explained in a 2008 article in the *Guardian*, "Without the great poet there would be no *liturgical, debauchery, besottedly, unhealthily, padlock, dismissive, terrific, embellishing, fragrance, didactic* or *love-lorn*. And certainly no *complacency*."

Alexander's count, which was apparently restricted to words not phrases, put Milton and his 630 neologisms ahead of **Ben Jonson** with 558, **John Donne** with 342, and **William Shakespeare** with a mere 229.[3] Such exact numbers underscores the problem of counting neologisms, because Shakespeare coined—and here's the rub—or popularized any number of additional words depending on the source you rely on, who is doing the counting, and the criteria used.

The Bard is also credited in the *Oxford English Dictionary* as being the first to use the terms *bedazzle, archvillain, fashionable, inauspicious, vulnerable, sanctimonious*, and *outbreak*. Whether or not those words were created by Shakespeare is up for debate, but he seems to have been the first to write them down. A May 2013 search of the online *OED* came up with 1,728 words (not words and phrases, but words) for which the Bard is given credit for "first use" ranging alphabetically from *abrook* (to endure, tolerate) to *yravish* (ravish). First use is different than coined or created because it simply acknowledges that this is the first evidence of a surviving record for use of that term, and over time this number is likely to go down rather than go up as earlier printed sources are uncovered and digitized to make the search easier.

The number of Shakespearean coinages has been a matter of speculation for decades and I have reserved a small bonus section in the back of this book to discuss the Bard's lexical box score. Numbers notwithstanding, when it comes to Shakespeare, there are a number of ways to look at his impact. According to the book *Coined by Shakespeare: Words and Meanings First Penned by the Bard* by Jeffrey McQuain and Stanley Malless, there are, for example, at least ten words commonly used in sports lingo that originate from the work of William Shakespeare. They are: *buzzer, negotiate, lackluster, undervalue, juiced, scuffle, vulnerable, rival, Olympian*, and *manager*. In *Shakespeare on Toast*, Ben Crystal rattles off these Bardisms: "Even-handed, far-off, hot-blooded, schooldays, well-respected are Shakespeare's too, as are lonely, moonbeam and subcontract."[4]

It seems to go deeper than single words but also to phrases and expressions that are now part of the fabric of everyday life. As Brenda James points out in her book *The Truth Will Out: Unmasking the Real Shakespeare*, "It may well be that no educated English-speaking person goes more than (at most) a few hours without using one or more words *coined by Shakespeare*, almost certainly without knowing it."[5]

Since the time of the Bard, the ability to create new words or even to be the first to use them has become tougher. But some standouts along the way to the present will be featured in this book, including many words or sayings that are in common use, names that are familiar to everyone—or what Shakespeare called *household words*, a term that makes its debut in the Saint Crispin's Day speech in *Henry V*.

> Old men forget: yet all shall be forgot,
> But he'll remember with advantages
> What feats he did that day: then shall our names.
> Familiar in his mouth as household words.

Acorns to Oaks

The question this raises is how do words make it into the realm of the household word at a moment when the language seems to have more than enough words to sustain itself. It is one thing to create a new word or catchphrase and quite another for one of your lexical offspring to find acceptance. As John Moore wrote in his book, *You English Words*, "The odds against a new word surviving must be longer than those against a great oak-tree growing from any given acorn."

The author of this book has created more than fifty new words and new definitions for old words and all but two of them have thus far failed to germinate and have been relegated to the category of nonce words, a lexical purgatory for words used rarely and in the context of their creator.

My two neologisms appear as entries in the body of this book. One is *word word* for a word that is repeated to distinguish it from a *seemingly* identical word or name (a *book book* to distinguish the prior work in question from an e-book), a term that now shows up in several major reference books. But my bigger success as a neologizer has been the word *demonym*. It was created to fill a void in the language for those common terms that define a person geographically—for example, *Angeleno* for a person from Los Angeles. I have used the term in several articles and books and was pleased to note in 2013 that it had 3,870,000 Google hits. Then in April 2013 the term was used by the American nonfiction master John McPhee in the *New Yorker*. It seems that he collects books on American place-names and demonym has become part of his natural vocabulary.[6]

Coined or Collected—Mind or Mined

A dilemma posed by the author of this book is the issue of words actually coined by a writer versus those the writer acquired from someone or someplace else but that they have been credited with.

In 1900, a writer named Leon Mead actually wrote to Mark Twain to ask him if he had coined any words. Twain replied that he knew of no words he had coined that had become part of the language, but that he had given currency to some that were already in use, particularly words and phrases he had extracted from the Western mines.

Mead responded, "I think it is safe to say that Mark Twain has not only popularized words and phrases which might have died but for his tonic treatment of them, but has coined others which have become familiar, at least in our vernacular." He added that the same may be said of Bret Harte (1836–1902), the American author and poet best remembered for his accounts of pioneering life in California who was getting his new words from those around him in locales like Poker Flat and Red Gulch.[7]

Twain's point about the mines was important and he would expand on it, elsewhere insisting that many of the words and phrases attributed to him were actually things he had heard on the Mississippi River and points west. To Twain the language created in the wake of the Gold Rush was the richest. He once wrote: "The slang of Nevada is the richest and most infinitely varied and copious that has ever existed anywhere in the world, perhaps, except in the mines of California in the early days. It was hard to preach a sermon without it and be understood."

Examples from Twain that came out of the mines and mining camp included *struck it rich*, which quickly applied to any human success; *up the flume*, signifying failure; *hard pan*, meaning a solid paying basis; *petered out*, which suggests a gradual decline and final suspension of resources; *grubstake*, the assistance given a new business enterprise on condition of a share in prospective or possible profits; *bonanza*, meaning sudden wealth or good fortune; and *squeal*, meaning to confess and betray companions. Twain is also credited by the *OED* with the first use in print of *blow up* (to lose self-control) in 1871, of *slop* (effusive sentimentality) in 1866, and of *sweat out* (to endure or wait through the course of) in 1876.

The issue of new words that are coined by the author vs. recording the words that are heard on the streets—or the mines and mining camps of the wild west or the inns and taverns of Stratford-on-Avon—applies to any writer who draws from the real life around him or her. As Leon Mead also pointed out, "The main secret of Dickens' popularity was that he knew his types; their counterparts were in real life. They talked the argot of the London slums, the bombast of the Old Bailey, the syco-phantic phrases of the counting-room, the cockney jargon of the slap-up swells."[8]

So the caveat issued with this book is that some of the coinages were second strikes.

Authorisms

A TO Z

A MAN GOT TO DO WHAT HE GOT TO DO. Phrase that appears in American novelist **John Steinbeck**'s (1902–1968) *The Grapes of Wrath* in chapter 18 when Casy says, "I know this—a man got to do what he got to do." This phrase is often attributed to John Wayne and to the lead character in the movie *Shane*, who utters lines similar to but not exactly this one.[1]

A MODEST PROPOSAL. Name for an outrageous proposal. The phrase is used commonly to describe heavy-handed satire. It comes from the name of such a satire with the full title *A Modest Proposal for Preventing the Children of Poor People in Ireland, from Being a Burden on Their Parents or Country, and for Making Them Beneficial to the Publick*, written by Anglo-Irish satirist, essayist, political pamphleteer, poet, and cleric **Jonathan Swift** (1667–1745), in which he suggests that the Irish eat their own children or sell them as food. Swift was Irish and deeply resented British policies toward the Irish and his insane proposal was an attack. In a letter to Alexander Pope in 1729 he wrote, "Imagine a nation the two-thirds of whose revenues are spent out of it, and who are not permitted to trade with the other third, and where the pride of the women will not suffer [allow] them to wear their own manufactures even where they excel what come from abroad: This is the true state of Ireland in a very few words."[2]

ABRICOTINE. Apricot-colored. A nonce word created by poet **Edith Sitwell** (1887–1964) and employed in one of her poems. Nonce words are words made up for a specific, usually one-time use in literary pursuits. Counting her book of poetry, the *OED* in which *abricotine* is listed, and its appearance here, it would seem among the rarest of words. However, the 2013 online edition of the *OED* contains no less than 4,419 nonce words of which this word is the first in alphabetical order. The last is *yogified*, a nonce word meaning to be treated in a yogic manner. It was created by **E. M. Forster** (1879-1970).[3]

ACCORDING TO HOYLE. According to the highest authority; done with strict adherence to the rules. Coined in this sense in 1906 by **O. Henry** (1862–1910), which was the pen name for William Sydney Porter, an allusion to the books of card and game rules written by Edmond Hoyle.[4]

AFGHANISTANISM. A term coined by **Jenkin Lloyd Jones** (1843–1919), a former member of the National Conference of Editorial Writers as well as columnist and editor of the *Tulsa Tribune*, to describe the journalistic practice of concentrating on problems in distant parts of the world while ignoring controversial local issues. He explained, "It takes guts to dig up the dirt on the sheriff, or to expose a utility racket, or to tangle with the governor. They all bite back and you had better know your stuff. But you can pontificate about the situation in Afghanistan in perfect safety. You have no fanatic Afghans among your readers. Nobody knows more about the subject than you do, and nobody gives a damn." [5]

AGEISM. Prejudice or discrimination based on one's age. A term coined by physician and author **Dr. Robert N. Butler** (1927–2010), who believed that as a society we should think about individual function, not age. Butler is known for his 1975 book *Why Survive? Being Old in America*, which won the Pulitzer Prize for General Nonfiction in 1976. He believed that society should confront ageism and work on constructive solutions to ameliorate it.[6]

AGNOSTIC. A term coined by English biologist and author (and grandfather of Aldous and Julian Huxley) **Thomas Henry Huxley** (1825–1895) in 1869 to indicate "the mental attitude of those who withhold their assent to whatever is incapable of proof, such as an unseen world, a First Cause, etc. Agnostics neither dogmatically accept nor reject such matters, but simply say agnostic—I do not know—they are not capable of proof." Huxley was apparently tired of being called an atheist when he created this distinction.[7]

AHA MOMENT. A sudden realization, inspiration, insight, recognition, or comprehension. When this word was added to the 2012 edition of *Merriam-Webster's Collegiate Dictionary*, much was made of the fact that television personality **Oprah Winfrey** had popularized the phrase in interviews with guests when moments of sudden insight occurred. The term actually made its debut in 1939 in the textbook *General Psychology*, written by **Lawrence Edwin Cole**, (1899-1974) in which he uses it to describe the moment of insight. The *OED* notes that Chaucer used "a ha" in this context in about 1386 in *The Nun's Priest's Tale*: "They cried, out! A ha the fox! and after him thay ran."[8]

ALL HELL BROKE LOOSE. This phrase originated in *Paradise Lost* by **John Milton** (1608–1674). At the end of book 4, the angel Gabriel asks Satan why he came alone and "Came not all Hell broke loose?" Milton created several other well-known demonic phrases: *better to reign in hell, than serve in heav'n* is his as is *pandemonium*.[9]

ALMIGHTY DOLLAR. American money as a tool of power, a term coined by American author and diplomat **Washington Irving**

(1783–1859). It appears first in a story of his called "The Creole Village" in 1836. "'The almighty dollar,' that great object of universal devotion throughout our land, seems to have no genuine devotees in these peculiar villages." Irving was the first American author to make a living from writing novels.[10]

ALOGOTRANSIPHOBIA. Fear of being caught on public transportation with nothing to read. Created in 1992 by novelist **George V. Higgins** (1939–1999), Martin F. Nolan, then editorial page editor of the *Boston Globe,* and Irish-born saloonkeeper Thomas Costello who had first "perceived a lacuna in our lexicon" regarding the problem. The three collaborated on the word, which was created from a combination of Greek and Latin. The Greek word *logos* was thought to be more mellifluous than the Latin *verbum,* and it also more specifically means a written rather than a spoken word. A full account of the creation of this term appears in the *Boston Globe* of September 14, 1972.

ALTRUISM. A theory of conduct that regards the good of others as the ultimate moral action. The term (French *altruisme,* derived from Latin *alter,* "other") was coined in the nineteenth century by French philosopher and writer **Auguste Comte** (1798–1857) and introduced into English usage by way of an October 1852 article by George Henry Lewes, published in the *Westminster Review.* Comte was the founder of positivism, a philosophical and political movement that enjoyed a wide diffusion in the second half of the nineteenth century. In the twentieth century, novelist Ayn Rand's decision (made in 1942, while completing *The Fountainhead*) to use *altruism* as her primary term for the moral tendencies that she found contemptible was occasioned by an encounter with Comte's ideas. Comte also gets credit for coining the term *sociology* when he divided all science into five great branches— astronomy, natural philosophy, chemistry, physiology, and sociology.[11]

AMBIVALENCY. The paradox in the human psyche that allows for the coexistence of contradictory feelings such as hate and love. Term created by **Sigmund Freud** (1856–1939), who borrowed it from the vocabulary of chemistry. The word was so new, indeed, that the 1930 edition of *Webster's New International Dictionary* lists it among New Words, at the front of that edition where it is defined: "*ambivalency* (Latin, *ambo,* 'both,' and valency, or *valence*): The quality or fact of being ambivalent specifically, in psychology, 'the presence of contrary feeling tones, associated with the same idea or object.'"[12]

AMERICAN CENTURY. Term coined by **Henry Luce** (1898–1967), the publisher of *Time, Life,* and *Fortune* magazines in an editorial in *Life* magazine, to refer to the economic, cultural, and military dominance of the twentieth century.

AMERICANESS. American author **James Fenimore Cooper**'s (1789–1851) failed attempt to create a word for an American woman as distinct from the male American. "Every true American and Americaness was expected to be at his or her post" appears in the 1838 debut of the short-lived term.[13]

ANCHOVY. A small fish of the herring family found off the European coasts, especially in the Mediterranean, where it is caught and prepared for export. It is known for its strong salty taste. The word comes from the Spanish *anchova* for small fish. It first appears in English when in **Shakespeare**'s *Henry IV, Part I,* Prince Hal has the servant Pero search the pockets of the drunken Falstaff and finds a bill for various items including "anchaues and sacke after supper." This is a prime example of a word Shakespeare is said to have coined but that he almost certainly picked up from common usage. Otherwise those attending the play would have been puzzled.*

ANECDOTAGE. The reminiscence period of old age. American historian, novelist, and film director **Rupert Hughes** (1872–1956) created this and a number of other new words including *dialectophobia* and *dialectophobes,* of the enmity and enemies to the use of dialect, and *viceversation,* a pedantic form for topsy-turvyism. He argued that these terms were "merely whimsical and of no earthly use."[14]

ANGRY YOUNG MAN/ANGRY YOUNG MEN. A group of British novelists, playwrights, and filmmakers who emerged in the 1950s and as a group expressed scorn and disaffection with the established social and political order of their country. Their impatience and resentment were especially aroused by what they perceived as the hypocrisy and mediocrity of the upper and middle classes. The movement was defined by **John**

---

* The anchovy may be one of the more literary fish as Charles Dickens wrote approvingly of anchovy paste. In 1856 in *Household Words* in an entry for June 28, he wrote "Anchovy Paste . . . and the whole stock of luxurious helps to appetite" and it appears as a repast several places in his writing including *Little Dorrit* where it is served on toast. Here is one of the simpler recipes for the paste:

8 ounces anchovies packed in oil, drained, coarsely chopped
2 tablespoons fresh white bread crumbs
1/2 cup butter
1 pinch ground cinnamon
1 pinch ground ginger
1 pinch ground black pepper

Directions: 1. Using a mortar and pestle, pound the anchovies and butter until they resemble a smooth paste. You could also use a food processor. 2. Stir in the bread crumbs, spices, and pepper and spoon the paste into a large ramekin. Cover and chill before serving.

Osborne's (1929–1994) play *Look Back in Anger*, which debuted in 1956. A press agent for the theater called Osborne "an angry young man." The term seems to have had its origin in 1951 with the publication of novelist, poet, journalist, academic friend of T. S. Eliot, **Leslie Paul**'s (1905–1985) autobiography, which he called *Angry Young Man*.

ANTHROPOPHAGINIAN. An adjective formed by **William Shakespeare** from *anthropophagi* (meat eaters, cannibals) for the sake of a formidable sound.

A-NUMBER-1. First-class, outstanding, first used in print in 1838 by **James Fenimore Cooper** in one of his novels about life at sea, *Homeward Bound*.

APPOINTMENT IN SAMARRA. Metaphor used to indicate the inevitability of death. The expression first shows up in a 1933 play by English dramatist and novelist **W. Somerset Maugham** (1874–1965) in which the servant to a merchant encounters Death in the marketplace at Baghdad and flees to Samarra to escape falling into his grip. Death then says, "I was astonished to see him in Bagdad, for I had appointment with him tonight in Samarra." The following year American novelist John O'Hara used the phrase to title *Appointment in Samarra*, probably his most famous and important work. Samarra is a real city in Northern Iraq and was the target of a major US assault in March 2006, as part of the War in Iraq, an action that occasioned several editorials in major newspapers to suggest that this was George W. Bush's appointment in Samarra.

APTRONYM. American columnist and wit **Franklin P. Adams** (1881–1960), well known by his initials F. P. A., coined this word for a name that sounds like its owner's occupation; for instance, William Rumhole, who was a London tavern owner. In Noah Jonathan Jacobs's *Naming-Day in Eden* we are told of a Russian ballerina named Olga Tumbelova. **Gene Weingarten**, a writer for the *Washington Post*, has coined *inaptronym* for a name that is ironic as opposed to appropriate, e.g., the late Cardinal Sin—Jaime Lachica Sin, the Roman Catholic Cardinal of Manila.

ARTFUL DODGER. A street thief or con artist; but also used as a nickname for someone who avoids work and responsibility. The term is an eponym for the nickname of a character in **Charles Dickens**'s (1812–1870) *Oliver Twist*, whose real name was Jack Dawkins but who was given this name in tribute to his skills as a pickpocket.[15]

ASPHALT JUNGLE. Any urban area regarded as a dangerous place where people are engaged in a struggle for survival. Coined by **George Ade** (1866–1944) in one of his "fables in slang" published in 1920: "After the newly arrived Delegate from the Asphalt Jungles had read a Telegram . . . he . . . sauntered back to the Bureau of Information." The term was popularized in *The Asphalt Jungle*, a 1949 novel by W. R. Burnett (1899–1982), about a jewel robbery, and in a popular 1950 film of the same title starring Marilyn Monroe.[16]

ASSASSINATION. The act of murder usually applied to the killing of a prominent person by sudden or secret attack, often for political reasons. The earliest known literary use of the word *assassination* is in **Shakespeare**'s *Macbeth*: "If th' Assassination Could trammell up the Consequence, and catch With his surcease, Successe."[17]

AVIATOR. The pilot of an airplane as distinguished from a balloonist or aeronaut. It first appears in the 1887 translation of French novelist **Jules Verne**'s (1828–1905) *The Clipper of the Clouds* (1887) in which the verb *aviated* also makes its debut. "Mr. Aviator, you who talk so much of the benefits of aviation, have you ever aviated?"[18]

AW-SHUCKS. To act bashfully; to say, "Aw, shucks."

 American author and journalist **Tom Wolfe** apparently was the first to turn this expression of humility into a verb in the November 1964 issue of *Harper's Bazaar.* "Up on the terrace ... the Secretary of the Interior of the United States, is sort of aw-shucksing around."

B

BABBITT. Charactronym for a conformist American businessman who, in the terms of the time of his creation, has traded his ethics and chivalry for a Buick. From the 1922 novel of the same name by **Sinclair Lewis** (1885–1951), who in 1930 became the first writer from the United States to be awarded the Nobel Prize in Literature. Babbitt became synonymous with the smug, narrow-minded, back-slapping businessman loathed by the social critics, especially H. L. Mencken, who wrote of him: "As an old professor of babbittry, I welcome him as an almost perfect specimen —a genuine museum piece. Every American

city swarms with his brothers . . . He is no worse than most, and no better; he is the average American . . . incarnate, exuberant and exquisite. Study him well and you will know what is the matter with the land we live in."[1]

The label was so popular that it soon spawned *babbittess, babbitian, babbittism, babbitless*, and *babbitry*. Alfred H. Holt points out in *Phrase Origins*: "Curiously enough, an earlier Babbitt, a real one, had given a word to the language, the name of a metal alloy he had invented."[2]

BACRONYM. A name so constructed that its acronym fits an existing word. The author of the term was retired navy commander and word hobbyist **Meredith G. Williams** (1924–2012) of Potomac, Maryland, who won the November 1983 contest for neologisms run by the *Washington Post*. The newspaper quoted Williams, who said it was the "same as an acronym, except that the words were chosen to fit the letters." A classic example of this is the Apgar score used to rate the health of newborns. It was initially named for Virginia Apgar who developed the test. But a decade later the bacronym APGAR was created in the United States as a mnemonic learning aid listing the key variables in the test: appearance, pulse, grimace, activity, and respiration.

BAD-MOUTH. To abuse verbally. Introduced by American writer and humorist **James Thurber** (1894–1961) in the April 5, 1941, *Saturday Evening Post*: "He bad-mouthed everybody."

BAD SEED. An evil child or person whose evilness is innate. The term is the title of the 1955 play by **Maxwell Anderson** (1888–1959) based on a book by William March about a little girl who murders as recreation. In both the novel and the play the evil child survives but when the film was made in 1956 by director Mervyn LeRoy, the Hays Code was still in effect—which dictated that crime could not pay—and the evil child is killed by a bolt of lightning.

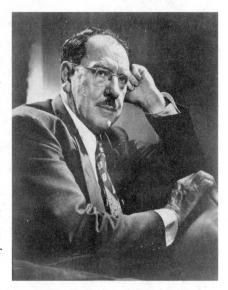

BANANA REPUBLIC. A politically unstable, undemocratic, and tropical nation whose economy is largely dependent on the export of a single limited-resource product, such as a fruit or a mineral. The pejorative term was coined by **O. Henry** in his 1904 collection of short stories entitled *Cabbages and Kings,* which he wrote in Honduras while he was evading embezzlement charges in the United States. He later went to jail for his crime.[3]

As John Soluri points out in his book *Banana Cultures: Agriculture, Consumption, and Environmental Change in Honduras and the United States*, "The tragically powerful metaphor has served as both an explanation of and a justification for the political conflicts, poverty, and U.S. interventions that were at the center of twentieth-century Central American history. Paradoxically, many people in the United States have distanced themselves from Central America by using bananas—the very commodity that has linked the two regions for more than a century—as a symbol for 'corrupt,' 'backward,' and 'underdeveloped' societies."[4]

BARDOLATRY. Worship of Shakespeare. A term of derision, it was created by Irish dramatist **George Bernard Shaw** (1856–1950) in 1901. Shaw followed it up with *bardolator* in 1903 and *bardolatrous* in 1905. His commentary on Shakespeare is voluminous and almost always negative—e.g., "With the single exception of Homer, there is no eminent writer, not even Sir Walter Scott, whom I can despise so entirely as I despise Shakespeare when I measure my mind against his."[5]

BARNACULAR. The quality of officialese coined by British journalist and man of letters **Ivor Brown** (1891–1974), who based the term "on the Dickensian family of Tite Barnacles who clung with such tenacity to official posts."

BASE BALL. A bat and ball game whose name is written as two words, a construction that is seldom used today but was dominant in the nineteenth century when it was introduced by **Jane Austen** (1775–1817) in *Northanger Abbey*, written in

1798 or 1799 but published in December 1817: "It was not very wonderful that Catherine [Morland], who had by nature nothing heroic about her, should prefer cricket, base ball, riding on horseback, and running about the country, at the age of fourteen, to books."

Although Austen appears to be the first to use the term in a literary context, a more recent discovery made by baseball historian David Block shows an even earlier allusion to the game in print. In 2013 Block discovered a 264-year-old English newspaper called the *Whitehall Evening-Post*. The issue of the newpaper in question has news of inmates attempting a jailbreak from Newgate Prison, and of a chestnut mare that disappeared from a local forest. On page 3, there is a small item. It reads:

> On Tuesday last his Royal Highness the Prince of Wales, and Lord Middlesex, played at Base-Ball, at Walton in Surry; and notwithstanding the Weather was extreme bad, they continued playing for several Hours.

The date of the game was September 12, 1749. [6]

BEAST WITH TWO BACKS. **Shakespeare**'s own copulatory metaphor, which debuts in *Othello*, act 1, scene 1: "I am one, sir, that comes to tell you your daughter and the Moor are now making the beast with two backs."

BEAT GENERATION. A group of young people, mostly writers and artists, who created a school of unconventional, nonconformist art, music, and writing. Their self-stereotype was antifashion and favored black clothing. One of their number, **John Clellon Holmes** (1926–1988), wrote of the term in the *New York Times Magazine* in November 1952: "It was the face of a Beat Generation . . . It was **[Jack] Kerouac** . . . who . . . several years ago . . . said, 'You know, this is really a *beat* generation.' The origins of the word beat are obscure, but the meaning is only too clear to most Americans. More than the feeling of weariness, it implies the feeling of having been used, of being raw. It involves a sort of nakedness of mind." Later Holmes reported that Kerouac added, "Beat means beatitude not beat up."[7]

BEATNIK. Term created by *San Francisco Chronicle* columnist **Herb Caen** (1916–1997) in his column of April 2, 1958, about a party for "50 beatniks." Caen was later quoted, "I coined the word 'beatnik' simply because Russia's *Sputnik* satellite was aloft at the time and the word popped out." The word caught on immediately with the public, which was looking for a word to describe this new breed of bohemians. Jack Kerouac, among others who used the term *beat* to describe themselves, did not like *beatnik*. Kerouac told biographer Ann Charters that he was "King of the Beats, but I'm not a Beatnik."[8]

In his book on American youth slang, *Flappers 2 Rappers*, Tom Dalzell says, "*Beatnik* must be considered one of the most successful intentionally coined slang terms in the realm of 20th century American English. *Sputnik*/beatnik led to a host of variations including *neatnik*, someone who is well dressed and well groomed; *Vietnik*, someone opposed to the war in Vietnam; and *peacenik*, for individuals who were antiwar. However, the term *no-goodnik*, a good-for-nothing, was coined by American humorist **S. J. Perelman** (1904–1979) in the *New Yorker* magazine in 1936.

BEDAZZLED. To be irresistibly enchanted, dazed, or pleased. A word that **Shakespeare** debuts in *The Taming of the Shrew*, act 4, scene 5: "Pardon, old father, my mistaking eyes, that have been so bedazzled with the sun that everything I look on seemeth green." Several of the websites that track the Bard's word have, in recent years, commented on the fact that a commercial product called the Bedazzler had come on the market and was usurping some of the dazzle from this word. The Bedazzler is a plastic device used to attach rhinestones to blue jeans, baseball caps, and other garments. One site commented, "A word first used to describe the particular gleam of sunlight is now used to sell rhinestone-embellished jeans."

BETTER HALF. Term for the female of the species coined by nineteenth-century feminist **Mary Livermore** (1820–1905) in her book *On the Sphere and Influence of Women*: "Regarding her as I do as the better half of humanity—with a more delicate and sensitive nature than man—with a more refined and spiritual organization—woman should be the conservator of public morals."[9]

BIBLE BELT. A derogatory label coined in 1925 by **H. L. Mencken** (1880–1956) following his coverage of the Scopes "monkey" trial in Dayton, Tennessee. Mencken applied the term to areas of the United States that were dominated by people who believed the Bible was literally true. While Mencken did not assign a specific geographic area to the term, he did use it for the rural areas of the Midwest and the South. He once designated Jackson, Mississippi, as the heart of both the Bible and Lynching Belts.[10]

BIBLIOBIBULI. Term coined by **H. L. Mencken** to describe those who are "drunk on books, as other men are drunk on whiskey or religion."

BIG BROTHER. British author **George Orwell**'s (1903–1950) term for an omnipresent government that relied on covert operations to monitor and modify the behavior of its citizens: "Big Brother is watching you." (One of George Orwell's six rules of good writing was never to use a metaphor, simile, or other figure of speech that you are used to seeing in print.)

BILLIONAIRE. The possessor of property worth a billion or more dollars. Coined by **Oliver Wendell Holmes Sr.** (1809-1894) in his 1861 novel *Elsie Venner: A Romance of Destiny*: "One would like to give a party now and then, if one could be a billionaire."

BIOGRAPHY. Restoration poet and critic **John Dryden** (1631–1700) coined this word in the preface to his translation of Plutarch in which he defined it as "the history of particular men's lives."

BIOPHILIA. Name of 1984 book by American biologist **E. O. Wilson** in which the term is created and defined as the "innate human urge to affiliate with other forms of life."

BIRTH CONTROL. Term created by **Margaret Sanger** (1879–1966), who founded the Planned Parenthood Federation of America and was in the forefront of the fight for women's reproductive rights. The term first appeared in her socialist-feminist periodical the *Woman Rebel* in 1914. In the same year Sanger wrote and published a pamphlet on methods of contraception, *Family Limitation*, which was based on her research on techniques and technologies available around the world.[11]

BITCH GODDESS. Success as seen through the prism of its negative consequences; any destructive obsession. Creation of pioneering American psychologist **William James** (1842–1910), who wrote in 1906: "A symptom of the moral flabbiness born of the exclusive worship of the bitch-goddess success." **D. H. Lawrence** (1895–1930) used the term to fine effect in *Lady Chatterley's Lover:* "He realized now that the *bitch-goddess* of success had two main appetites: one for flattery, adulation, stroking and tickling such as writers and artists gave her, but the other a grimmer appetite for meat and bones."[12]

BLABBERMOUTH. First used by **John Steinbeck** in his 1936 novel *In Dubious Battle*: "One minute he's a blabbermouth kid."

BLACK HOLE. An invisible object in outer space formed when a massive star collapses from its own gravity. A black hole has such a strong pull of gravity—within a certain distance of it—nothing can escape, not even light. Coined by **John A. Wheeler** (1911–2008) at a conference in New York in 1967, Dr. Wheeler, seizing on a suggestion shouted from the audience, hit on the name *black hole* to dramatize this dire possibility for a star and for physics. The black hole "teaches us that space can be crumpled like a piece of paper into an infinitesimal dot, that time can be extinguished like a blown-out flame, and that the laws of physics that we regard as 'sacred,' as immutable, are anything but," he wrote in his 1999 autobiography, *Geons, Black Holes, and Quantum Foam: A Life in Physics*

BLACK POWER. Created by African American writer **Richard Wright** (1908–1960) as the title for his 1954 book on

Africa's Gold Coast and its enormous potential. The term was adopted as a slogan for a broader movement in support of civil rights and political power for black people. The movement was especially prominent in the United States in the 1960s and 1970s and closely associated with the Student Nonviolent Coordinating Committee. Wright's books tended to have strong, memorable titles— *Uncle Tom's Children*, *Black Boy*, and *Native Son*.

BLADDERCLOCK. The use of one's bladder as an alarm clock; drinking the right amount of water the night before to get up at a specified time in the morning. Coinage of **Bill Sherk**, author of *Brave New Words*, a brilliant collection of fresh mintings from Canada.

BLATANT. The word first appeared in 1596, as part of poet **Edmund Spenser**'s (1552–1599) poem "The Faerie Queene." The invented word describes a horrible monster known as the Blatant Beast, which is why the word's first definition is "noisy and particularly vulgar." The Blatant Beast as it appears in the poem is "a dreadful fiend of gods and men, ydrad"; the type of calumny or slander. He was begotten of Cerberus and Chimera, and has a hundred tongues and a sting; with his tongues he speaks things "most shameful, most unrighteous, most untrue," and with his sting "steeps them in poison." Sir Artegal pursues him and Sir Calidore muzzles the monster, and draws him with a chain to Faerie Land. The beast breaks his chain and regains his liberty. Having coined the word *blatant*, Spenser never uses it except as a modifier for his monster. It is probably derived from the provincial word *blate*, meaning to bellow or roar.[13]

BLUE-COLLAR. See WHITE-COLLAR.

BLURB. A brief descriptive paragraph or note of the contents or character of a book, printed as a commendatory advertisement on the wrapper, or jacket, of a newly published work. The word was coined in 1907 by American author and humorist **Gelett Burgess** (1866–1951), who employed a book jacket

embellished with a drawing of a pulchritudinous young lady whom he facetiously dubbed Miss Belinda Blurb. It was later given a full definition in his 1914 comic dictionary *Burgess Unabridged*:

> *Blurb*, 1. A flamboyant advertisement; an inspired testimonial. 2. Fulsome praise; a sound like a publisher ... On the "jacket" of the "latest" fiction, we find the blurb; abounding in agile adjectives and adverbs, attesting that this book is the "sensation of the year."

The term gained such immediate acceptance that all friendly endorsements became known as blurbs. In the early 1950s there was a move to replace the term with the euphonious *jacketism* (alluding to the dust jacket of a book), but it was an ill-fated move.[*]

BOBOS. American journalist **David Brooks**'s compressing of "bourgeois bohemians" used to describe former social rebels who are now well-heeled and self-indulgent and featured in his 2000 book *Bobos in Paradise: The New Upper Class and How They Got There*. Brooks explained the gist of the term and the book as his discovery of an "America in which the bohemian and the bourgeois were all mixed up. It was now impossible to tell an espresso-sipping artist from a cappuccino-gulping

---

[*] Paul McFedries, who maintains the Word Spy website and has written the book *Word Spy: The Word Lover's Guide to New Words,* notes that *blurb* is "a relatively rare example of a slang term that makes the leap into mainstream use." He adds, "I'm on a personal mission to keep another of Mr. Burgess' coinages afloat: *tintiddle*, 'a witty retort, thought of too late.' Please do me a huge personal favor and slip this word into a conversation or two this weekend."

banker. And this wasn't just a matter of fashion accessories. I found that if you investigated people's attitudes toward sex, morality, leisure time, and work, it was getting harder and harder to separate the antiestablishment renegade from the pro-establishment company man."

BOOBOISIE. A segment of the general public composed of uneducated, uncultured persons. It is a blend of *boob* + *bourgeoisie*, coined by **H. L. Mencken** in 1922. An individual American who was not too bright was termed *Boobus Americanus* by Mencken, the reporter, editor, columnist, and author of many books including *The American Language: An Inquiry into the Development of English in the United States.*

BOOM. As a verb meaning to burst into prosperity or suddenly rise in popularity, this term was introduced by **Joseph B. McCullagh** (?–1896), a St. Louis newspaper editor, in July 1878: "The fact is, the Grant movement for a third term of the presidency, is booming." When he was later asked to explain the word, McCullagh replied, "I cannot recall how I came to use it except that, while on the gunboats of the Mississippi River during the war I heard pilots say of the river when rising rapidly and overflowing its banks, that it was 'booming.' The idea I wished to convey was that the Grant movement was rising— swelling. The word seemed to be a good one to the ear, and I kept it up. The word was generally adopted about a year afterward. I used it as a noun, after a while and spoke of 'the Grant boom.' "[14]

BOREDOM. One could be a bore before 1852, but this word for tedium did not enter the English language until 1852, when **Charles Dickens** used it six times in his ninth novel, *Bleak House*. The French word *ennui* was in full play when Dickens coined *boredom*. The first citation for ennui in the *OED* is a quote from 1661 that decries the fact English did not have words that fully expressed the French words *naiveté*, *bizarre*, and *ennui*.[15]

BOSWELL. Eponym for a companion who witnesses and records what another person does. The term alludes to the relationship between James Boswell and Samuel Johnson, whose life Boswell recorded. **Oliver Wendell Holmes** coined the term in his 1858 work *Autocrat of the Breakfast Table* when he wrote: "Every man his own Boswell." A key adopter of the term was Arthur Conan Doyle, who, in *The Adventures of Sherlock Holmes*, has Holmes say to his assistant Watson: "Stay where you are. I am lost without my Boswell."

BOXER. A prizefighter; a pugilist. A term that makes its debut in English novelist **Henry Fielding**'s (1707–1754) *Joseph Andrews* in 1742: "A stout Fellow, and an expert Boxer."

BRAINWASHING. A forcible indoctrination to induce someone to give up basic political, social, or religious beliefs and attitudes and to accept contrasting regimented ideas. The term created by American journalist, author, and intelligence agent **Edward Hunter** (1902–1978) first appeared in a dispatch that he wrote for the *Miami Daily News* on September 24, 1950. It was used again by him in other dispatches and his 1951 book *Brain-Washing in Red China: The Calculated Destruction of Men's Minds*. The term replaced earlier terms like *mind control* and *menticide*, and must be regarded as one of the more successful coinages of the post–World War II era. A 2013 Google search yielded more than 5.5 million hits.[16]

BRAVE NEW WORLD. A phrase that originated in **Shakespeare's** *The Tempest*, act 5, scene 1, as part of a speech by Miranda:

> O wonder!
> How many goodly creatures are
>   there here!
> How beauteous mankind is! O
>   brave new world,
> That has such people in't.

It became the title for **Aldous Huxley's** (1894–1963) dystopia, which was published in 1932 and depicted a soulless world of totalitarian cultural control in which, for instance, the works of William Shakespeare are banned. *Brave new world* has become a catchphrase for any social or technological change that is reminiscent of the world depicted by Huxley in his novel, i.e., a world that is regimented, soulless, and sterile—a true dystopia. When Huxley's work was paired with George Orwell's *1984* and Arthur Koestler's *Darkness at Noon*, the books formed a trilogy of cautionary tales for mid-twentieth-century readers.

BRICK. None other than English novelist **William Makepeace Thackeray** (1811–1863) created this term for a merry citizen with many friends but little social standing; a jolly good citizen content in his or her mediocrity. He first employed it in the sentence: "He's a dear little brick."

BRILLIG. Four o'clock in the afternoon: a time according to English writer **Lewis Carroll** (1832–1898) when you begin broiling things for dinner.

BROBDINGNAGIAN. That which is huge, gigantic, vastly oversized. It comes from **Jonathan Swift**'s 1726 satire *Gulliver's Travels* in which Brobdingnag was a country of giants, twelve times the size of normal humans.

BROMIDE AND SULPHIDE. Words coined by **Gelett Burgess** in his humorous 1906 essay *Are You a Bromide? The Sulphitic Theory Expounded and Exemplified*, which explains "the terms 'bromide' and 'sulphite' as applied to psychological rather than chemical analysis." The *bromide*, according to Burgess, "does his thinking by syndicate. He follows the main-traveled roads, he goes with the crowd." The *sulphite*, on the other hand, is unconventional, original, everything that the bromide is not.

BROMIDIC. That which is common or conventional. Burgess stated in *Are You a Bromide?* that "the Bromide can't possibly help being bromidic."

BROUHAHA. An uproar, a to-do. From the French but blended into English in 1890 by **Oliver Wendell Holmes** in

Over the Teacups: "I enjoy the *brouhaha* . . . of all this quarrelsome menagerie of noise-making machines."

BUNBURY. An imaginary person used as a bogus excuse for visiting a place or avoiding work, it has become a fictional eponym for a spurious alibi. The Irish writer and poet **Oscar Wilde** (1854–1900) wrote in *The Importance of Being Earnest,* "I have invented an invaluable permanent invalid called Bunbury, in order that I may be able to go down into the country whenever I choose." Before the book is finished he has extended Bunbury's reach to other parts of speech. "Now that I know you to be a con-firmed Bunburyist I naturally want to talk to you about Bunburying."

BUTTERFINGERS. **Charles Dickens** used the term in his 1836 *The Pickwick Papers* (more properly called *The Posthumous Papers of the Pickwick Club*): "At every bad attempt at a catch, and every failure to stop the ball, he launched his personal displeasure at the head of the devoted individual in such denunciations as 'Ah, ah!—stupid'— 'Now, butter-fingers'—'Muff'— 'Humbug'—and so forth."

BUTTINSKY. Faux eponym for person who interrupts, who butts in. Created by American author **George Ade**, who wrote some of his stories in slang. His 1902 *The Girl Proposition* says, "The Friend belonged to the Buttinsky Family and refused to stay on the Far Side of the Room."

CALIFORNIA. Coined in 1510 by the Spanish novelist **Garci Rodríguez de Montalvo** in the book *Las Sergas de Esplandián,* in which the name was applied to an imaginary island where there was an abundance of precious stones, gold, and women. "Know that on the right hand of the Indies there is an island called California very close to the side of the Terrestrial Paradise; and it is peopled by black women, without any man among them, for they live in the manner of Amazons."

CALYPSO. The term is certainly older in its indigenous culture but it was **Aldous Huxley** who according to the *OED* imported it to a literary context in 1934. "The tunes to which these songs are sung is always some variant of an old Spanish air called Calypso; the words are home-made and topical."[1]

CATBIRD SEAT. A position of control and mastery, often stated as "sitting in the catbird seat." The term was popularized in the 1940s by American baseball broadcaster and journalist **Red Barber** (1908–1992), who would use it, for example, to describe a batter with a count of three balls and no strikes, or a pitcher with a big lead. The term has long been attributed to Barber: even though he denied having created it, he explained how he once "bought" it. In his 1968 biography *Rhubarb in the Catbird Seat*, Barber tells the story of playing penny ante poker in Cincinnati with friends, and sitting for hours unable to win a hand. Then he related, "Finally, during a round of seven-card stud, I decided I was going to force the issue. I raised on the first bet, and I raised again on every card. At the end, when the showdown came, it was between a fellow named Frank Cope and me. Frank turned over his hole cards, showed a pair of aces, and won the pot. He said, 'Thank you, Red. I had those aces from the start. I was sitting in the catbird seat.' I didn't have to be told the meaning. And I had paid for it. It was mine."

CATCH-22. The working title for Joseph Heller's (1923–1999) modern classic novel about the mindlessness of war was *Catch-18*, a reference to a military regulation that keeps the pilots in the story flying one suicidal mission after another. The only way to be excused from flying such missions is to be declared insane, but asking to be excused for the reason of insanity is proof of a rational mind and bars being excused. Shortly before the appearance of the book in 1961, Leon Uris's bestselling novel *Mila 18* was published. To avoid numerical confusion, Heller and his editor decided to change *Catch-18* to *Catch-22*. The choice turned out to be both fortunate and fortuitous as the *22* more rhythmically and symbolically captures the double duplicity of both the military regulation itself and the bizarre world that Heller shapes in the novel. ("'That's some catch, that Catch-22,'" observes Yossarian. 'It's the best there is,' Doc Daneeka agrees.")

During the more than half century since its literary birth, *catch-22*, generally lowercased, has come to mean any predicament in which we are caught coming and going, and in which the very nature of the problem denies and defies its solution. So succinctly does *catch-22* embody the push-me-pull-you absurdity of modern life that the word has become the most frequently employed and deeply embedded allusion from all of American literature often by those with no idea where the term came from.

CELL. The structural, functional, and biological unit of all organisms. English naturalist Robert Hooke (1635–1703) coined the term *cell* after viewing slices of cork through a microscope. The term came from the Latin word *cella,* which means "storeroom" or "small container." He documented his work in the *Micrographia,* written in 1665.

CHAPLINESQUE. Resembling the comic physical style of actor **Sir Charles Spencer,** known as **Charlie Chaplin** (1889–1977) and renowned for his portrayal of a down-trodden little man with baggy trousers, bowler hat, and cane. Irish playwright **George Bernard Shaw** turned the comedian's name

into an adjective in 1921 and Hart Crane used it for the name of one his most famous poems in 1933.[2]

CHEESECAKE. Appeared in *Time* magazine on September 17, 1934: "Tabloid and Heartsmen go after 'cheesecake'—leg-pictures of sporty females."

CHICKADEE. Common name for the black-cap chickadee, a bird common to North America and in the same group as the titmouse. The name appears to have been coined by American author **Henry David Thoreau** (1817–1862) who used it as early as 1839. It appears in *Walden* in 1854: "The chickadee lisps amid the evergreens."

CHINTZY. Originally this word meant to be decorated or covered with chintz, a calico print from India, or suggestive of a pattern in chintz. It was extended to mean unfashionable, cheap, or stingy, coming from none other than Mary Ann Evans, better known by her pen name **George Eliot** (1819–1880) who wrote in a letter in 1851: "The effect is chintzy and would be unbecoming."[3]

CHORTLE. Blend of *chuckle* + *snort* created by **Lewis Carroll** in *Through the Looking-Glass:* "'O frabjous day! Callooh! Callay!' He chortled in his joy."

CHUG-A-LUG. This onomatopoeic exhortation to hastily consume beer also represents, in the words of the *OED*, "a glugging, chugging, or gobbling sound, esp. that of a person consuming a drink in large gulps." The term was introduced, again according to the *OED*, in 1903 by the American Western adventure novelist **Zane Grey** (1872–1939) in the book *Betty Zane:* "Presently the silence was groken [*sic*] by a long, shrill, peculiar cry. 'Chug-a-lug, chug-a-lug, chug-a-lug-chug.' 'Well, it's a turkey, all right,' . . . remarked Colonel Zane."

CO-ED. Short for coeducation—any coeducational institution or system. **Louisa May Alcott** (1832–1888) wrote in *Jo's Boys:* "Never liked *co-ed*." The line is uttered by a boy named Adolphus "Dolly" Pettingill, who objected to eating with girls.

COINED THE WORD/ COINED THE PHRASE. The notion of coining words in the manner of minting coins seems to have started with Elizabethan writer **George Puttenham** (1529–1590) in 1589 in *The Arte of English Poesie* in which he complains of "young schollers not halfe well studied" who "seeme to coigne fine wordes out of the Latin." In French a *coigne* is a die used to stamp money. Shakespeare, the greatest coiner of them all, also referred to the coining of language in *Coriolanus*, 1607: "So shall my Lungs Coine words till their decay."

COJONES. Testicles in the allegorical sense, representing courage and tenacity. Imported from Spanish by **Ernest**

Hemingway (1899–1961) in his 1932 nonfiction bullfighting opus *Death in the Afternoon:* "It takes more cojones," he wrote, "to be a sportsman where death is a closer party to the game."

COLD WAR. In terms of the specific ideological conflict between the United States and the Soviet Union, the term was first used by **Herbert Bayard Swope** (1882–1958) of the *New York World* in speeches he wrote for financier and industrialist **Bernard Baruch** (1870–1965). Baruch said in a speech in South Carolina on April 16, 1947: "Let us not be deceived— today we are in the midst of a cold war." Afterward, Swope noted that the press picked up the phrase and it soon became a part of everyday speech. However, using the term to describe an indirect conflict, the *Oxford English Dictionary* credits **George Orwell** in 1945 describing "a state which was in a permanent 'cold war' with its neighbours."

COMSTOCKERY. Strict censorship of materials considered obscene. Named for Anthony Comstock, a United States postal inspector and politician who was dedicated to ideas of Victorian morality. The term was coined by **George Bernard Shaw** in 1905 after Comstock had alerted the New York police as to the content of Shaw's play *Mrs. Warren's Profession*. Shaw remarked in a bylined piece in the *New York Times* of September 26, 1905, that "Comstockery is the world's standing joke at the expense of the United States. Europe likes to hear of such things. It confirms the deep-seated conviction of the Old World that America is a provincial place, a second-rate country-town civilization after all." Comstock thought of Shaw as an "Irish smut dealer."

CONSPICUOUS CONSUMPTION. Spending for the sake of show, a concept introduced and so labeled by **Thorstein Veblen** (1857–1929) in his 1899 *Theory of the Leisure Class* in which he wrote: "Conspicuous consumption of valuable goods is a means of reputability to the gentleman of leisure." Less recalled today, Veblen also described the end product of conspicuous consumption: "The need of conspicuous waste ... stands ready to absorb any increase in the community's industrial efficiency or output of goods."

COTTON WOOLIES. British novelist, short story writer, poet, fighter pilot, screenwriter, and children's book author **Roald Dahl** (1916–1990) created this generic term for what modern children are not interested in reading about. He used the term in an interview that appeared in an article about his writing in the *Hartford Courant:* "I write of nasty things and violent happenings because kids are themselves that way ... Kids are too tough to read about little cotton woolies."

COUNTERCULTURE. American author, scholar, and critic **Theodore Roszak** (1933–2011) created this term for the social upheavals of the 1960s into the mainstream in his work *The Making of a Counter Culture.* The book was published in 1969, three weeks after the Woodstock Festival, which was then and still is emblematic of Roszak's label.

CROWDSOURCING. Term created by *Wired* magazine writer **Jeff Howe** and editor **Mark Robinson** that initially referred to when a company outsourced a job using a group of people (usually volunteers or people who receive a small compensation) gathered through an open call on the Internet to tap into an enthusiastic knowledge base that can—under ideal conditions—even outperform experienced professionals.[4]

CRYPTEX. A word created by novelist **Dan Brown** in *The Da Vinci Code* to describe a portable vault concealing the secret location of the legendary Holy Grail.

CUPERTINO EFFECT. Term that describes what happens when a computer automatically "corrects" your spelling into something wrong or incomprehensible. The name originates from an early spellchecking program's habit of automatically correcting the word "cooperation" (when spelled without a hyphen) into "Cupertino," the name of the California city in which Apple has its headquarters. The term was created by Tom Chatfield, author of *Netymology: From Apps to Zombies—A Linguistic Celebration of the Digital World*. Chatfield discussed the effect in the April 1, 2013, issue of the online *BBC News Magazine* where he wrote: "One of my favorite Cupertinos was my first computer's habit of changing the name 'Freud' into 'fraud'—or, more recently, of one phone's fondness for converting 'soonish' into 'Zionism.'"[5]

CYBERIAN. Demonym for an inhabitant of cyberspace or Cyberia, a term invented by **Howard Rheingold** in 1991 in his book *Virtual Reality: Exploring the Brave New Technologies of Artificial Experience and Interactive Worlds—From Cyberspace to Teledildonics*. "I've heard the cyberians at one VR software vendor refer to the head-mounted display … as 'the face-sucker.'"

CYBERSPACE. Novelist **William Gibson** invented this word in a 1982 short story, but it became popular after the publication of his sci-fi novel *Neuromancer* in 1984. He described cyberspace as "a graphic representation of data abstracted from banks of every computer in the human system. Unthinkable complexity." In 1996 Gibson wrote an essay that appeared in the *New York Times Magazine* in which he said, "I coined the word *cyberspace* in 1991 in one of my first science fiction stories and subsequently used it to describe something that people insist on seeing as sort of a literary forerunner of the Internet. This being so, some think it remarkable that I do not use E-mail." He did admit to being an avid browser of the World Wide Web.[6]

D

DADDYKNOWSBESTISM. Coined by American newspaper columnists **Joseph Alsop** and **Stewart Alsop** in an article criticizing the American government for telling the American people less than one-tenth of what they ought to know about the atomic bomb.[1]

DAIQUIRI. The cocktail that is named for a district in Cuba was first acknowledged in print in 1920 in **F. Scott Fitzgerald's** (1896–1940) *This Side of Paradise.* Fitzgerald probably did not coin the term or invent the drink, but he went a long way toward introducing it to a larger audience in the 1920 novel in which a character begins the night by ordering "four double daiquiris" from an "old jitney waiter." In what could have been a cautionary tale for the alcoholic Fitzgerald, the character then sees a man turn into a purple zebra, "a figment of his besotted imagination."*

DEBUNK. Word created by novelist, biographer, and former advertising copywriter **William E. Woodward** (1874–1950) for the process of exposing false claims. He used it in his 1923 novel *Bunk*, in which he also created the term *debunker* and *debunking*. Others would later debunk Woodward's biographies of George Washington and Ulysses S. Grant that attempted to debunk great figures of history but were generally dismissed as exercises in cynicism and little else.[2]

DEMIMONDE. **Alexandre Dumas** (1802–1870), best known for his historical novels of high adventure, created this term in 1855 for the title of his play, *Le Demi-Monde*. The term *demimonde* (literally, half world) originally designated a class of fallen society women—women with a past who are therefore compromised. Over time the definition came to be much broader, including all women of loose morals who lived at the

---

* The drink consumed by Fitzgerald and his fictional characters was probably as follows:

2 ounces light rum
1 ounce fresh lime juice
¼ –½ ounce simple syrup

Add all ingredients except the garnish with ice in a shaker. Shake well to combine. Strain into a chilled cocktail glass and garnish.

edge of respectable society and, by extension, the men—royal, aristocratic, bourgeois, and bohemian—who frequented that shadowy world. Dumas complained that his word had been taken over and was devoid of its original meaning. C. S. Lewis examined this word and its transformation in his *Studies in Words* and warned: "Aspiring neologists will draw a moral. Invent a word if you like. It may be adopted. It may even become popular. But don't reckon on its retaining the sense you gave it and perhaps explained with great care."[3]

DEMONYM. Term created by **Paul Dickson** and initially presented in the form of a dictionary definition:

> **demonym** *n.* **1.** [from Greek *demos* "the people" or "populace" + -*nym* "name"] A name commonly given to the residents of a place or a people. The names Briton, *Midwesterner, Liverpudlian, Arkansawyer,* and *Parisienne* are all *demonyms.* **2.** An adjective of residence. It may be the same as the noun (*Haitian*) or it may be different (*Swede* for the noun, *Swedish* for the adjective).[*]

---

[*] The earliest form of this word was *domunym.* After publishing several articles on the subject, including one that appeared in the March 1988 *Smithsonian* magazine, I received several letters noting that I could use some help with my neologism. The most compelling case was made by George H. Scheetz, then director of the Sioux City (Iowa) Public Library and member of the American Name Society and the North Central Name Society, who has actually made a study of words with a -*nym* ending. Scheetz wrote:

> All but two historically occurring words ending in -*nym* actually end in -*onym,* and all but approximately six percent are formed from Greek root words. In other words, the Latin root *dom-* (from *domus*), more correctly forms *domonym.* However, the Greek root is already in use as a combining form, *domato-* (from *domatos*), which forms *domatonym.* Literally, both these combinations mean "a house name." The names Tara and The White House are domatonyms. So Scheetz must be credited with a major assist with this word.

DINOSAUR. A long-extinct race of reptiles, some of gigantic size. Their name was coined and bestowed on them in 1841 by **Sir Richard Owen** (1804–1892), who explained the name in the *Proceedings of the British Association for the Advancement of Science* in 1842. In that article, Owen wrote, "The combination of such characters, some, as it were, from groups now distinct from each other, and all manifested by creatures far surpassing in size the largest of existing reptiles, will, it is presumed, be deemed sufficient ground for establishing a distinct tribe or suborder of Saurian Reptiles, for which I would propose the name of Dinosauria." The name came from the Greek *deinos,* meaning fearfully great, and *sauros,* meaning lizard.[4]

DIRT PUNCHER. Farmer or farm worker, a term created by **Eugene O'Neill** (1888–1953) for his play *The Rope,*

Eugene O'Neill and Carlotta Monterey O'Neill

which was first performed in 1918. Near the end of the play, the prodigal son tells how he feels about life on a farm and what his father's farm means to him. There he says, "I don't want no truck with this rotten farm. You kin have my share of that. I ain't made to be no damned dirt puncher—not me! And I ain't goin' to loaf round here more'n I got to, and when I goes this time I ain't never comin' back. Not me! Not to punch dirt and milk cows. You kin have the rotten farm for all of me. What I wants is cash—regular coin yuh kin spend—not dirt." O'Neill also inverted the term to form a verb *to punch dirt*.

DISMAL SCIENCE. A term coined by Scottish writer, essayist, and historian **Thomas Carlyle** (1795–1881) to describe the discipline of economics. It was inspired by T. R. Malthus's gloomy prediction that population would always grow faster than food, dooming mankind to unending poverty and hardship.

DISQUALIFY. To deprive of the qualifications required for some purpose; to render unqualified. Though there were variations on the word *disqualify* before being first used by **Jonathan Swift** in 1733, Swift appears to be the first to use this term in print. He also later uses it in referring to himself. In a letter to Alexander Pope in 1736: "My common illness is of that kind which utterly disqualifies me for all conversation; I mean my Deafness."[5]

DOORMAT. As a metaphor applied to a person upon whom other people "wipe their boots." First used in this sense by

Charles Dickens in *Great Expectations*: "She asked me and Joe whether we supposed she was door-mats under our feet, and how we dared to use her so."

DOUBLETHINK. The ability to accept as equally valid two entirely contrary beliefs. **George Orwell** wrote in *1984*: "His mind slid away into the labyrinthine world of doublethink. To know and not to know, to be conscious of complete truthfulness while telling carefully constructed lies, to hold simultaneously two opinions which cancelled out, knowing them to be contradictory and believing in both of them, to use logic against logic, to repudiate morality while laying claim to it, to believe that democracy was impossible and that the Party was the guardian of democracy."

DRACULA. Name for the king of the vampires, invented by **Bram Stoker** (1847–1912) in the 1897 novel of this name, used allusively to denote a grotesque or terrifying person.

DRAGON LADY. Any powerful villainous woman, from the character of the same name created in 1936 by **Milt Caniff** (1907–1988) for his *Terry and the Pirates* comic strip. She makes her first appearance in the strip of September 6 with the introductory line: "Mongolian Princess, My Eye! That woman is the *Dragon Lady!*"

DRECK. Rubbish, worthless debris, a Yiddishism that the *OED* lists as having been introduced by **James Joyce** (1882-1941) in *Ulysses,* "Farewell. Fare thee well. *Dreck!*"[6] This was probably in wide use long before Joyce but there is no earlier example in the context of written English.

DROODLE. A riddle in the form of a simple line drawing—a blend of drawing and riddle. The term was invented and copyrighted by writer-cartoonist **Roger Price** (1918–1990), who published a book entitled *Droodles* in 1953. Droodle is a true lexical rarity in that it is not listed in the *OED* and neither is his other creation, the *mad lib,* which he created in 1953 with Leonard Stern.

DYMAXION. The term is used in referring to construction and design by **R. Buckminster Fuller** (1895–1983): as "yielding the greatest possible efficiency in terms of the available technology, 'doing the most with the least.'" The word was created by blending the word *dynamic* and the concept of *maximum service.* The word was not coined by Fuller. He explained in a 1969 private communication to the editors of the *Oxford English Dictionary* that the word was coined for him in 1929 by his business associates as a "word-portrait" of him and his work. They were concerned to form a euphonious word of four syllables based on words that occurred in Fuller's own description of his prototype (Dymaxion) house, viz, *dy*(namism), *max*(imum), and *ion*. When Fuller wrote his treatise on *dymax-ion*, *Nine Chains to the Moon*, Carl Wiegman reviewed the book for the *Chicago Tribune* and noted, "It would be a lot more dymaxion if Mr. Fuller did not have a literary style that almost drives a reader crazy."[7] [*]

DYSTOPIA. See entry for **UTOPIA.**

---

[*] Fuller attained a level of eponymous glory in the name *buckminsterfullerene*, which is officially described as "an extremely stable form of carbon whose molecule consists of 60 carbon atoms joined together as a truncated regular icosahedron of 12 pentagons and 20 hexagons, forming a symmetrical spheroidal structure suggestive of the geodesic dome." The geodesic dome is one of Fuller's inventions.

E

EARFUL. As much talk as one's ears can listen to at one time; a large quantity; a strong reprimand. The first appearance is in a 1917 story by American sports columnist and short story writer **Ring Lardner** (1885–1933).[1]

EBONICS. African American English when seen as a dialect with features derived from West African languages rather than a nonstandard variety of English. The name and the theory made its public debut on January 26, 1973, by **Robert L. Williams**, an African American and professor of psychology at Washington University in St. Louis. Its first published appearance was in a 1975 book edited by Williams, *Ebonics: The True Language of Black Folks*. Williams fashioned the term *Ebonics* by combining *ebony* (for black) and *phonics* (for the scientific study of speech sounds), and he used Ebonics to identify the variety of English spoken by many black Americans as a language or at least a dialect of its own rather than merely "bad English." Aside from some Afrocentrists, however, everyone else continued to call it black English or, in a more scholarly vein, African American vernacular English.

ECDYSIAST. Word coined by American author and journalist **H. L. Mencken** for a striptease. The term was based on a request from a very popular practitioner. As Mencken recounted in the second volume of *The American Language*, in 1940 he received a letter from Georgia Sothern asking him to create a word that would mean striptease but would contain a more elegant sound and sense: "I am a practitioner of the fine art of strip-teasing ... In recent years, there has been a great deal of uninformed criticism leveled against my profession ... I feel sure that if you could coin a new and more palatable word to describe this art, the objections to it would vanish and I and my colleagues would have easier going. I hope that the science of semantics can find time to help the verbally underprivileged members of my profession. Thank you."

Mencken chronicled the difficulty he encountered in searching for a synonym for stripteaser. "The word moltician comes to mind, but it must be rejected because of its likeness to mortician ... A resort to the scientific name for molting, which is ecdysis, produces both ecdysist and ecdysiast. Then there are suggestions in the names of some of the creatures which practice molting. The scientific name for the common crab is *Callinectes hastastus*, which produces *callinectian*. Again, there is a family of lizards called the *Geckonidae*, and their name produces *gecko*. Perhaps your advisers may be able to find other suggestions in the same general direction."

Mencken settled on *ecdysiast*.[2]

ECONOLOGY. The blend of the words *economy* and *ecology*. The link between the two is based on the growing awareness of the impact of human activities on the environment. The word was minted as a typographical error by the teletype operator transmitting a column by **Frank Worbs** in the *Beaver County Times*, published in Pennsylvania. The column discussed the relationship between economy and ecology. A typo is a typo and nothing was made of the error for a month. But on February 17, 1972, Worbs wrote a follow-up column entitled "New Word Coined" in which he declared *econology* to be a legitimate new word with real-world application to environmental problems.[3]

EEYORE. A pessimistic person and by extension *eeyorish* for gloomy, or pessimistic. Several words and character names coined by **A. A. Milne** (1882–1956) in the Winnie-the-Pooh series have come into general use. The most prominent example may be the donkey, Eeyore, whose gloominess is notorious in the stories. A typical exchange between Eeyore and Pooh occurs when Pooh says "good morning" to Eeyore, and Eeyore responds, "Good morning, Pooh Bear . . . If it *is* a good morning . . . Which I doubt." Eeyorish was added to the *OED* in 2003 along with *muppet* (taken from the children's TV show *Sesame Street*, to mean a foolish person).

EGGCORN. Name for the substitution of a word or phrase for a word or words that sound similar or identical in the speaker's dialect but that still make sense—e.g., *old timer's disease* for *Alzheimer's disease, mute point* for *moot point, ex-patriot* for *expatriate,* and the author's favorite *doggy-doggy world* for *dog-eat-dog world. Eggcorn* was coined by linguist and coauthor of *The Cambridge Grammar of the English Language* **Geoffrey Pullum** in 2003 as the soundalike substitution of *acorn.*

EGGHEAD. A 1918 letter from American author and poet **Carl Sandburg** (1878–1967) introduced this derogatory term for an intellectual. Sandburg indicated that Chicago newspapermen used the term to refer to highbrow editorial writers out of touch with the common man. In the 1950s, the word surged in popularity when Democrat Adlai Stevenson was branded with the term in his unsuccessful presidential campaigns.

EMPEROR'S NEW CLOTHES. A metaphor for human folly from the name of a fairy tale by Danish author **Hans Christian Andersen** (1805–1875) about two weavers who promise their emperor a new suit of clothes that is invisible to those who are unfit for their positions, stupid, or incompetent. Since no one wanted to admit he could not see the clothes and admit to being a fool, the clothes were praised. But when the emperor parades before a child in his new clothes, the child cries out, "But he isn't wearing anything at all!"

EPHEMERALIZATION. The 1960 creation of **R. Buckminster Fuller** for doing more with less, specifically referring to machinery becoming smaller and lighter over time.

EREWHON. Title of a **Samuel Butler** (1835–1902) novel published anonymously in 1872. The title is also the name of a country, supposedly discovered by the protagonist. In the novel, it is not revealed in which part of the world Erewhon is, but it is clear that it is a fictional country. Butler meant the title to be read as the word *nowhere* backward even though the letters *h* and *w* are transposed; therefore Erewhon is an anagram of *nowhere*. In the preface to the first edition of his book, Butler specified: "The author wishes it to be understood that Erewhon is pronounced as a word of three syllables, all short—thus, E-re-whon." Nevertheless, the word is occasionally pronounced with two syllables as "air – one."

ERGOTIZE. To quibble, wrangle. This rare word was coined from the Latin word *ergo* by Scottish novelist, poet, essayist, and travel writer **Robert Louis Stevenson** (1850–1894).[4]

ESCAPEE. Term that makes its debut in 1875 in **Walt Whitman**'s (1819–1892) in his memoirs of the war in which he writes of "Southern Escapees."

ESCAPIST. In the sense of seeking distraction from reality, the 1933 creation of British essayist and novelist **C. S. Lewis** (1898–1963).

ESOTERICA. Term for esoteric objects or products; esoteric details. American poet of light verse **Ogden Nash** (1902–1971) introduced the word in a poem published in 1929 with the line: "The postal authorities of the United States of America Frown on Curiosa, Erotica and Esoterica."

ET TU, BRUTE. The last words of Julius Caesar as imagined by **William Shakespeare**. Literally, "And you, Brutus?" Used in a modern context as a sarcastic remark after a minor act of betrayal. It comes from the play *Julius Caesar* and alludes to the moment in 44 BC when Julius Caesar was murdered by a group of senators led by Marcus Brutus, who had previously been Caesar's close friend. In the play Caesar begins to fend off the attack but resigns himself to his fate when he sees that his friend has betrayed him:

Caesar: Doth not Brutus bootless kneel?
Casca: Speak, hands, for me! [They stab Caesar.]

Caesar: Et tu, Brute? Then fall, Caesar! [Dies.]
Cinna: Liberty! Freedom! Tyranny is dead!⁵

ETH. A member of an ethnic group, one who displays ethnicity, a subject for study by ethnographers and ethnologists. Coined by American author and music critic **Herbert Kupferberg** (1918–2001) in his article "Confessions of an Eth" in *Parade* magazine in reaction to the 1,076-page *Harvard Encyclopedia of American Ethnic Groups.*

EUCATASTROPHE. Word coined by English writer, poet, philologist, and university professor **J. R. R. Tolkien** (1892–1973) in 1944 for a sudden or unexpected favorable turn of events, especially in a narrative, such as a surprise happy ending. *Eucatastrophe* was defined by Tolkien in his 1947 essay "On Fairy-Stories" as the "good catastrophe, the sudden joyous 'turn' . . . it is a sudden and miraculous grace . . . a fleeting glimpse of Joy." He first wrote of the eucatastrophe in 1944 as "the sudden happy turn in a story which pierces you with a joy that brings tears." In 1947 he expanded on the theme applying it to Christianity: "The Birth of Christ is the eucatastrophe of Man's history. The Resurrection is the eucatastrophe of the story of the Incarnation."⁶

EUGENICS. Coined in 1883 by **Sir Francis Galton** (1822–1911), British anthropologist and cousin of Charles Darwin, from a Greek word meaning "well born." Galton perceived it as a moral philosophy to improve humanity by encouraging the ablest and healthiest people to have more children.

PAUL DICKSON

EUTHANASIA. A gentle and easy death and by extension the act of purposely killing or helping someone die. It was first coined by **Francis Bacon** (1561–1626) in 1605 from Greek *eu* (good) and *thanatos* (death).

EUTRAPELIA. Clean mirth, a jest without a jeer, laughter without scorn, wit without malice, a joke without offense to one's neighbor. A word fashioned from the Greek by **Anselm Kroll**, a minister from La Crosse, Wisconsin. He tried valiantly to get others to adopt the concept in a crusade that pushed for the dawning of a new day of humor without barbs. "What a lovely world it will be when its clever folk cease to strive to be satirical or sarcastic, and resolve to be eutrapeleous."[7]

EYESORE. **William Shakespeare** coined this word for something that is offensive to the eye. In *The Taming of the Shrew*, Baptista demanded, "Doff this habit, shame to your estate, an eyesore to our solemn festival!" The term was invoked with proper acknowledgment to its coiner in 2005 when plans were unveiled to build a massive metal shed in Stratford on Avon as a temporary home for the Royal Shakespeare Theatre. It was immediately dubbed the Rusty Shed.[8]

F

FACTOID. Term created by **Norman Mailer** (1923-2007) in 1973 for a piece of information that becomes accepted as

a fact, although it is not actually true; or an invented fact believed to be true because it appears in print. Mailer wrote in *Marilyn:* "Factoids ... that is, facts which have no existence before appearing in a magazine or newspaper, creations which are not so much lies as a product to manipulate emotion in the Silent Majority."*

---

* Lately *factoid* has come to mean a trivial fact. That usage makes it a *contranym* (also called a Janus word) in that it means both one thing and its opposite, such as cleve (to cling or to split), sanction (to permit or to punish), and citation (a commendation or a summons to appear in court.)

FAQ. Initialism for *frequently asked questions*, a term in common use on Internet home pages. Attributed to **Eugene N. Miya**, researcher at NASA, who is said to have coined the term in ca. 1983 documents circulated to Usenet groups on the history of the space program.

FASHIONISTA. A person employed either in the creation or promotion of high fashion, by extension a devotee of the fashion industry. It can be used sardonically for someone obsessed by fashion. This word was created by writer **Stephen Fried** in his 1993 book *Thing of Beauty: The Tragedy of Supermodel Gia*, referring to a specific group of fashion insiders and devotees. The word is a play on Sandinista with the *–ista* suffix to imply "following." In 1999 the word was added to the *OED* and it continued to appear everywhere along with copy-cat words ending in –ista. Then in April 2013, Fried published a seventeen-paragraph mea culpa in the *Atlantic* entitled, "I Apologize for Inventing the Word 'Fashionista' 20 Years Ago," in which he said of his neologism: "Twenty years ago, I apparently changed language forever. I published a book that unleashed upon an unsuspecting public a single word of terrifying power and controversy . . . I suppose I should apologize to all users of language for my crime against nomenclature. I could also apologize to my wife, a writer and my editor, who lobbied loudly against the word when I invented it—and later came to believe that if we had only copyrighted it, we'd be fabulously wealthy by now."

Fried's apologia was published online and immediately attracted comments such as this one from a person named Carson: "This is the longest and most fulsome humble brag I can remember coming upon. It has to go in the humble-brag hall of fame and in the U.S. Dept. of Weights and Measures as the standard by which all future humble-brags are henceforth measured."[1]

FEMINIST. One who advocates social, political, and all other rights of women equal to those of men. Created by **Alexander Dumas** in 1873 as feministe and translated as feminist by G. Vandenhoff and identified in his translation as a neologism "The feminists [Vr.feministes] (excuse this neologism) say, with perfectly good intentions, too: All the evil rises from the fact that we will not allow that woman is the equal of man."[2]

FILM NOIR. First used (and presumably coined) by French critic **Nino Frank** (1904–1988) in 1946 to describe certain American B movies characterized by surreal settings, bold use of black and white, and visual contrast. The term has been clipped and extended to use as the adjective *noir* for anything akin to the films so described—a noir dream, mood, novel, etc.

FIRE-WATER. Liquor; ardent spirits. A word introduced by **James Fenimore Cooper** in *The Last of the Mohicans* through the observations of the character Natty Bumppo, the wilderness scout known as Pathfinder among the English and as Hawkeye among the Mohicans. "The Dutch landed, and gave my people the *fire-water*; they drank until the heavens and the earth seemed to meet, and they foolishly thought they had found the Great Spirit."

PAUL DICKSON

FLIBBERTIGIBBET. As a verb meaning to gad about frivolously; to play the flibbertigibbet (from the Middle English *flepergebet*). In 1921 **John Galsworthy** (1867–1933) turned it into a verb, which netted him a separate entry in the *OED* because he wrote: "His daughter would flibberty-gibbit all over the place like most young women since the War."

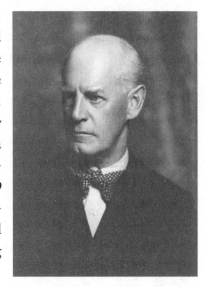

FLOWER POWER. Slogan created by American poet **Allen Ginsberg** (1926–1997) while encouraging antiwar protesters to embrace nonviolent rebellion. Ginsberg was a poet and one of the people who inspired the sixties counterculture. He was one of the most articulate voices of the beat generation, and his poem "Howl" is considered one of the most influential poems of the post–World War II era.[3]

FNORD. Term first used in **Robert Anton Wilson**'s (1932–2007) trilogy *The Illuminati Papers* to mean a propaganda work used to condition the masses from a very young age to respond with fear and anxiety. Over time the term has come to mean anything out of context that also has a surreal element. Fnords find comfort in offbeat web pages and places like the *Urban Dictionary* where definitions abound. A merciful few examples:

Fnord is a little pufflike cloud you see at 5 pm.

Fnord lives in the empty space above a decimal point.

Fnord is the 43 1/3rd state, next to Wyoming.

Fnord is the blue stripes in the road that never get painted.

Fnord is the empty pages at the end of the book.

Fnord uses two bathtubs at once.

FOMA. Harmless untruths, intended to comfort simple souls. They make you feel good and are the basis for US novelist **Kurt Vonnegut**'s (1922–2007) fictional religion Bokononism. Examples of common *fomas*: (1) Prosperity is just around the corner. (2) Don't worry. You'll get back together.

FOURTH ESTATE. Traditional name for the press and nowadays called the media. Although it is believed that the term was coined by **Edmund Burke** (1729-1797), the earliest recorded use of the term Fourth Estate to refer to the press is in 1787 when **Thomas Carlyle** wrote in his book *On Heroes, Hero-Worship, and the Heroic in History*: "Burke said there were Three Estates in Parliament; but, in the Reporters' Gallery yonder, there sat a Fourth Estate more important far than them all."

FRAK. A faux curse word created by writer **Glen A. Larson** for the original television series *Battlestar Galactica*. The word was mostly overlooked back in the seventies series but has become more and more commonly used in the twenty-first century in places ranging from sitcoms to coffee mugs. The emergence of the verb *frack* (short for the extraction process of hydraulic fracturing) has given new life to the term.

FRANKENSTEIN. A monster who is out of control. It derives from the name of Victor Frankenstein, who in **Mary Shelley**'s (1797–1851) 1818 romance *Frankenstein* constructed a human monster from an accumulation of human body parts and endowed it with life. In 2005 the *Oxford English Dictionary* added an entry for *Frankenstein food* as food that has been genetically modified or irradiated (also called *Frankenfood*).

FREAKONOMICS. For *freak economics*, a clever meld word coined by economist **Steven D. Levitt** and journalist **Stephen J. Dubner** in their 2005 book *Freakonomics: A Rogue Economist Explores the Hidden Side of Everything*. It's economics based on conventional wisdom, common sense, and numbers. Much of freakonomics confirms what we have long suspected—for example, that political candidates who have a lot of money to finance their campaigns are still out of luck if no one likes them—but it is still enlightening when stated in economic terms.

FREELANCE. One who sells services to employers without a long-term commitment to any of them; an uncommitted independent, as in politics or social life. The word is not recorded before **Sir Walter Scott** (1771–1832) introduced it in *Ivanhoe*, which, among other things, is often considered the first historic novel in the modern sense. Scott's freelancers were mercenaries who pledged their loyalty and arms for a fee. This was its first appearance: "I offered Richard the service of my Free Lances, and he refused them—I will lead them to Hull, seize on shipping, and embark for Flanders; thanks to the bustling times, a man of action will always find employment."[4]

FRENEMY. A blend of *friend* and *enemy* coined in 1953 by the American journalist **Walter Winchell** (1897–1972). "Howz about calling the Russians our Frienemies [*sic*]." Can refer to either an enemy disguised as a friend or to a friend who is "a person with whom one is friendly, despite a fundamental dislike or to a friend who is simultaneously a competitor and rival."

FRIENDING. The act of befriending, a term coined by **Shakespeare** in *Hamlet*, act 1, scene 5:

> And what so poor a man as Hamlet is
> May do, to express his love and friending to you.

In *The Shakespeare Key*, a book published in 1879, the authors Charles and Mary Cowden Clarke make the point that this overlooked coinage could be adopted by the larger language as a word implying "friendly feeling." With the advent of the social network Facebook in 2004, *friended* became widely adopted. Two other words from the Clarkes' list appear later in this lexicon: *irregulous* and *smilet*.[5]

FRUMIOUS. Blend of *fuming* and *furious* created and applied by **Lewis Carroll** beginning in 1871 in *Through the Looking-Glass* with the warning: "Beware the Jubjub bird, and shun the frumious Bandersnatch!"

FUDGE. This exclamation of contempt made its literary debut in Anglo-Irish novelist **Oliver Goldsmith**'s (1730–1774) *The Vicar of Wakefield* describing the very impolite behavior of Mr. Burchell, who at the conclusion of every sentence would cry out *fudge*.[6]

FUTURE SHOCK. A term created by **Alvin Toffler** for his 1970 book of the same name to describe a certain psychological state of individuals and entire societies where there is the perception of there being "too much change in too short a period of time." A key element of this state was "information overload," and he painted a picture of people who were isolated and depressed, cut off from human intimacy by a relentless fire hose of messages and data barraging them.

G

G-MEN. Agents of the Federal Bureau of Investigation, so called by **Walter Winchell** after the term that was used by Machine Gun Kelly to describe FBI agents as "government men."

GALUMPHING. **Lewis Carroll**'s word for a way of "trotting" downhill, while keeping one foot farther back than the other. This enables the *galumpher* to stop quickly. Generally believed to be a blend of *gallop* and *triumph,* the word first appears in the poem about the Jabberwocky, from *Through the Looking-Glass.* In modern application the term has been used to mean "to move clumsily" at one extreme and "to prance in triumph" at the other.

GAMESMANSHIP. The art of winning games by using various ploys and tactics to gain a psychological advantage; how to win without really cheating. The term was the creation of **Stephen Potter** (1900–1969) in 1947 in his book *The Theory and Practice of Gamesmanship or The Art of Winning Games*

Without Actually Cheating. Through *Gamesmanship,* Potter introduced the facetious use of the *-manship* suffix, which spawned a number of other -manship words, such as *brinkmanship* (first coined by Adlai Stevenson at the height of the Cold War). Potter went on to expand the concept into the social realm with *Lifemanship,* published in 1950 and then *One-upmanship,* published in 1952, which gave the language the word *one-upmanship* and the condition of being *one up.*

GARGANTUAN. From **François Rabelais's** (1490–1553) sixteenth-century series of novels entitled *Gargantua and Pantagruel,* a satirical story about a giant and his son.

GENE. The basic physical unit of heredity, a term coined by Danish botanist and—by extension of his own term—geneticist **Wilhelm Johannsen** (1857–1927) in 1909 in his book *Elements of the Exact Heredity (Elemente der exakten Erblichkeitslehre).* The term was created to be neutral by not tying to any given theory of heredity. He later combined it with the root *type* to form the word *genotype* and it was later used as the basis for other terms up to and including *genome* (a full set of chromosomes).[1]

GENTLEMAN FARMER. A country gentleman engaged in farming, usually on his own estate; by extension, a man of independent means who farms chiefly for pleasure rather than income. The concept first appeared in print in **Henry Fielding's** *Tom Jones* in 1749: "My Father was one of those whom they call a Gentleman Farmer. He had a little Estate of about 300 shillings a Year."

GENTRIFICATION. The process of middle-class or affluent people moving into and rebuilding deteriorating urban areas, often displacing poorer residents. The term was created by British sociologist **Ruth Glass** (1912–1990) in 1964 when she wrote: "One by one, many of the working class quarters of London have been invaded by the middle-classes—upper and lower. Shabby, modest mews and cottages—two rooms up and two down—have been taken over, when their leases have expired, and have become elegant, expensive residences ... Once this process of 'gentrification' starts in a district it goes on rapidly until all or most of the original working-class occupiers is displaced and the whole social character of the district is changed."

GILDED AGE. The period following the Civil War, roughly from the end of Reconstruction in 1877 to the turn of the twentieth century. The term was coined by **Mark Twain** and essayist-editor **Charles Dudley Warner** (1829–1900) in *The Gilded Age: A Tale of Today*. They satirized what they believed to be an era of serious social problems, greedy schemes, and vulgar extravagances obscured by a thin layer of gold.

GLOBAL VILLAGE. The concept advanced by Canadian communications theoretician **Marshall McLuhan** (1911–1980) that the globe has been contracted into a single village by electronic technology—radio and television, for starters—with the instantaneous movement of information from every quarter to every point at the same time.[2]

GLOBALIZATION. Coinage of Harvard professor **Theodore Levitt** (1925-2006), which he debuted in a 1983 *Harvard Business Review* article "The Globalization of Markets." His concept was that business was becoming globalized, which he defined as the changes in technology and social behaviors that allow multinational companies like Coca-Cola and McDonald's to sell the same products worldwide. In his sweeping style, he said, "Gone are accustomed differences in national or regional preferences."[3]

GLOT. A person who cannot bear to waste anything. Scottish-born journalist, poet, and scholar **Alastair Reid** first used it in his imaginative *Ounce, Dice, Trice*. See also GNURR and POOSE.

GNURR. **Alastair Reid**'s word for the substance that over time collects in the bottoms of pockets and the cuffs of trousers.

GOALLESS. American poet **Emily Dickinson** (1830–1886) from her poem "No Man Can Compass a Despair":

No Man can compass a Despair—
As round a Goalless Road.

A cluster of nonce words ending with –*less* (*postponeless* for that which cannot be put off or averted; *reduceless* for that which cannot be reduced; and *reportless* for that which is not worthy of or receiving notice) achieve listing in the venerable

OED because—or despite the fact that—they appear only in the poems of Emily Dickinson. *

GOBBLEDYGOOK. This term was coined by US Representative **Maury Maverick**, D–Texas (1895–1954), a grandson of the Samuel Maverick whose personality and presence gave us the name for one who is "independently minded." Maury Maverick was chairman of FDR's Smaller War Plants Corporation during World War II. *Gobbledygook* is Maverick's name for the long high-sounding words of Washington's red-tape language. "Just before Pearl Harbor, I got my baptism under 'gobbledygook' ... its definition: talk or writing which is long, pompous, vague, involved, usually with Latinized words. It is also talk or writing which is merely long."[4] It was first used in writing in a memo dated March 30, 1944, banning "gobbledygook language" and mock threatening and saying that "anyone using the words activation or implementation will be shot." Maverick explained that the term alluded to the noise of a turkey "always gobbledy gobbling and strutting with ludicrous pomposity."

GONZO. Crazed; having a bizarre style—especially as a modifier of the word *journalism* when referring to a purposely exaggerated rhetorical style. American slang expert Tom Dalzell supplies the etymology: "Although coinage is credited to US journalist and author **Bill Cardoso**, close friend and partner in adventure with the late **Hunter S. Thompson** (1937–2005) the dust jacket to Cardoso's collected essays

---

* A question that arises with nonce words is do they lose their nonceness now that they appear here. For that matter, will *nonceness* now appear in the *OED* because this could be its debut in print?

claims only that he is 'the writer who inspired Dr. Hunter S. Thompson to coin the phrase Gonzo journalism. Thompson first used the term in print and the term is irrevocably linked with him in the US." He used the term to great effect in *Fear and Loathing in Las Vegas:* "There was no avoiding the stench of twisted humor that hovered around the idea of a gonzo journalist in the grip of a potentially terminal drug episode being invited to cover the National District Attorneys' Conference on Narcotics and Dangerous Drugs."[5]

GOOD BAD BOOK. A term coined by English author and mystery novelist **G. K. Chesterton** (1874–1936) and later

adopted by George Orwell who defined it in his essay "Good Bad Books" as "the kind of book that has no literary pretensions, but which remains readable when more serious productions have perished." He divided these books into two further categories: escape literature, and other works "quite impossible to call 'good' by any strictly literary standard." Orwell also wrote of the genre: "One can be amused or excited or even moved by a book that one's intellect simply refuses to take seriously."

GOOGLE. In his weekly *Washington Post* column of March 1, 2012, **Gene Weingarten** wrote that few companies are as

George Ade

protective of their corporate name as Google. He continued, "The company is proud of its unusual name, which it says was coined in 1997 by its co-founders Larry Page and Sergey Brin in an accidental mis- spelling of the mathematical term 'googol.' It's not a verb, Google says, and never was, and using it as such violates the company's trademark."

"So," Weingarten continued, "imagine my surprise when I got an e-mail from a reader named Ed Lloyd, who had happened upon 'google' used as a verb in a collection of short stories published in 1942. In a story called 'Single Blessedness,' humorist **George Ade** wrote this: 'Charley Fresh—who regards himself as the irresistible captivator— googles his way among the girls for six nights a week and is known as a 'lady's man.'"

Weingarten concluded that from its context, Ade appeared to be using *google* to mean "unctuously ingratiate oneself with the opposite sex," but it could also be explained as meaning oogle and may have gotten a boost from the song "Barney Google (with the Goo Goo Googly Eyes)."

GOOSE-STEPPER. A dupe of conformity. **H. L. Mencken** introduced it in 1923 in his *Prejudices: Third Series* in an essay entitled "On Being an American," containing a typically Menckenesque blast of invective aimed at the American people: "The most timorous, sniveling, poltroonish, ignominious mob of serfs and goose-steppers ever gathered under one flag." The term had earlier roots as the original goose-steppers were from the British army, and the practice of marching without bending one's knees was used in training troops for balance.

GOTHAM. One of New York's most enduring nicknames, *Gotham* is Anglo-Saxon for "Goat Town," and comes from a town called Gotham (GOAT-um) in Lincolnshire, England, which was famous for tales of its stupid residents. Gotham was applied to New York City by **Washington Irving** and others in the 1807 *Salmagundi; or the Whim-Whams and Opinions of Launcelot Langstaff, Esq. and Others*. Lexicographer Barry Popik adds, "*Salmagundi* lampooned New York culture and politics in a manner much like today's *Mad* magazine." It was in the November 11, 1807, issue that Irving first attached the name Gotham to New York City and it was he that first called a native of that city a *Gothamite*.

GRANFALLOON. Any large, amorphous organization without real identity. Coined by American writer **Kurt Vonnegut**, who added, "Other examples of granfalloons are the Communist Party, the Daughters of the American

Revolution, the General Electric Company, the International Order of Odd Fellows—and any nation, anytime, anywhere." He introduced the term in the 1963 science fiction novel, *Cat's Cradle,* in which Vonnegut described the term as referencing a false *karass,* another Vonnegutian neologism referring to "a proud and meaningless association of human beings."

GREATEST GENERATION. Term created by journalist **Tom Brokaw** in his 2004 book of the same title to describe the cohorts who grew up during the Great Depression and went on to fight World War II. Brokaw described them as "the greatest generation any society has ever produced," arguing that they did not fight for fame and recognition rather because it was the right thing.

GREMLIN. Coined by the Royal Naval Air Service sometime during World War I, this word was made known by a

 children's book called *The Gremlins: A Royal Air Force Story,* written in 1943 by **Roald Dahl**. According to the story, a *gremlin* is a small creature that causes mechanical problems in aircraft. Since 1943, gremlins were blamed by Allied aircraft personnel for various mechanical and engine problems during World War II. The name was bestowed on a subcompact car by American Motors, but given the name's association with

mechanical problems it was replaced by the name Spirit in 1978.

GROK. To understand intuitively or by empathy; to establish rapport with. It was the creation of American science fiction writer **Robert A. Heinlein** (1907–1988) and made its debut in his 1961 novel *Stranger in a Strange Land*. "Smith had been aware of the doctors but had grokked that their intentions were benign." Heinlein also begot the *grokker* for one who understands. A favorite expression of Trekkies (ardent followers of the *Star Trek* television series) was "I grok Spock"—an allusion to one of the story's more complex characters.

GROUPTHINK. Term coined by social psychologist **Irving Janis** (1918-1990) in 1972 to describe what occurs when a group makes faulty decisions because group pressures lead to a deterioration of "mental efficiency, reality testing, and moral judgment." Groups affected by *groupthink* ignore alternatives and tend to take irrational actions that dehumanize other groups. A group is especially vulnerable to groupthink when its members are similar in background, when the group is insulated from outside opinions, and when there are no clear rules for decision making.[6]

GRUNTLED. Back formation of disgruntled meaning to be satisfied, content. It seems to have made its debut in 1938 in English humorist **P. G. Wodehouse's** (1881–1975) *The Code of the Woosters*: "He spoke with a certain what-is-it in his voice, and I could see that, if not actually disgruntled, he was far from being gruntled."

HAPPY HUNTING GROUNDS. The afterlife in the spiritual world of the Mohicans and other Indian tribes written about in 1826 by **James Fenimore Cooper**: "A young man has gone to the happy hunting grounds!" The next recorded user of the term was Washington Irving, adding to what Charles L. Cutler called its "literary aura."[1]

HARD-BOILED. Hardened, hardheaded, uncompromising. A term documented as being first used by **Mark Twain** in 1886 as an adjective meaning "hardened." In a speech he alluded to *hard-boiled*, hidebound grammar. Apparently, Twain and others saw the boiling of an egg to harden the white and yolk as a metaphor for other kinds of hardening.[2]

HEART OF DARKNESS. The evil subconscious that lurks inside human nature. The term was created by **Joseph Conrad** (1857–1924), a Polish author who wrote in English. In his 1902 story of the same name, the narrator searches for a man named Kurtz, a cruel white trader who lives deep in the jungle.

Joseph Conrad

HEAVY METAL. Highly amplified, harsh-sounding rock music with a strong beat, characteristically using violent or fantastic imagery. The term was adopted as a musical reference by *Creem* writer **Lester Bangs** (1948-1982) who began using it in the mid-seventies, taking the term from passages of William Burroughs's 1959 novel *Naked Lunch*.[3]

HEEBIE-JEEBIES. A feeling of uneasiness or nervousness; the jitters often transmitted from one person to another. Coined by American cartoonist **William De Beck** (1890–1942) in his comic strip *Barney Google*. The term debuted in 1923 in the *New York American*: "You dumb ox—why don't you get that stupid look offa your pan—you gimme the heeby jeebys!"* It was not until its second appearance in the comic that the term was given its final spelling: "31,000 shares! Worthless stock of 'the Belgian Hair Tonic Company' wiped out! Every cent I had in the world . . . It gives me the heebie jeebies."[4]

HEFFALUMP. Child's word for elephant that debuted in 1926 in **A. A. Milne**'s *Winnie-the-Pooh:* "He would go up very quietly to the Six Pine Trees now, peep very cautiously into the Trap, and see if there *was* a Heffalump there." The *OED* notes that the term is "now commonly in adult use."

HELL HATH NO FURY LIKE A WOMAN SCORNED. An abbreviated yet famous line coined by playwright and poet **William Congreve** (1670–1729) in 1697. The entire quote reads "Heaven has no rage like love to hatred turned, Nor hell a fury like a woman scorned," spoken by Perez in act 3, scene 2, *The Mourning Bride.*

HIGHBROW/LOWBROW. Distinction between intellectual elite and those who shun higher culture in favor of that which is popular and easily accessible. Opera is *highbrow*; popular music is *lowbrow*. The distinction is based on phrenology, in which having a high brow is seen as evidence of a larger brain, hence higher intellect. First applied to cultural taste and proclivity by US author, writer, and journalist **Will Irwin** (1873–1948) in a series of articles in the *New York Sun* in 1902.

---

* Pan = face, in the slang of the period.

HIGH-TONED. Adjective created by **Sir Walter Scott** to mean "nobly elevated."

HIPPISM. A philistine's resentment of a curiosity about the meaning of words. This term was coined by conservative American author and commentator **William F. Buckley Jr.** (1925–2008) after reading an attack on I. Moyer Hunsberger's *Quintessential Dictionary* by a Tampa, Florida, librarian named Joseph Hipp.

HOLISMO. Exaggerated holism; the belief that holistic medicine is a panacea. The word was created by **Fitzhugh Mullan**, MD, in response to the "outpouring of holism" offered by friends and acquaintances when he was seriously ill. The word made its debut in Mullan's article, "The Rising of Holismo," in *Hospital Physician* magazine.

HOLON. Word coined by Hungarian British author and journalist **Arthur Koestler** (1905–1983). He used it to describe an entity that is itself a *whole* but simultaneously *part* of a larger whole, in an infinite series, such that each entity is neither whole nor part, but a whole/part, or *holon*.

HOMINIST. **George Bernard Shaw**'s 1903 antonym to *feminist*: "One who advocates for men the rights and privileges conventionally accorded to women."

HONEY TRAP. A ploy in which an attractive person, usually a woman, lures another, usually a man, into revealing information; by extension, a person employing such a ploy. The term first came into play in 1974 in novelist **John le Carré**'s *Tinker, Tailor, Soldier, Spy*: "You see, long ago when I was a little boy I made a mistake and walked into a honey-trap."[5]

HONKY TONK. A tawdry roadhouse with a jukebox, a dance floor, and a bar. The term already existed but did not become a common term until **Carl Sandburg** used it in his *American Songbook* in 1927 in reference to the blues: "It was moaned by resonant moaners in honky tonks of the southwest."

HONORIFICABILITUDINITATIBUS. Meaning "the state of being able to achieve honors," this twenty-seven-letter word coined by **Shakespeare** in his comedy *Love's Labour's Lost* is a testament to the Bard's own linguistic skills. It has been posited that this is the longest word in the English language with alternating consonants and vowels.[6]

HOOTCHY-KOOTCHY. A provocative dance, associated with the dancer Little Egypt at the World's Columbian Exposition of 1893. The first appearance of the term in print is from an 1898 column by American humorist **Finley Peter Dunne** (1867–1936).

HUB. Boston as seen as the point around which the universe turns, a long-lived conceit drawn by **Oliver Wendell Holmes** in *The Autocrat of the Breakfast-Table:* "Boston State-House is the hub of the solar system. You couldn't pry that out of a Boston man, if you had the entirety of all creation straightened out for a crow-bar." Over time the metaphor was extended and Boston became the Hub of the Universe, and the term still lives on especially in sports reporting. Holmes is also credited with coining the term *Boston Brahmin*, a nickname for the wealthy enlightened class of Boston's mid-nineteenth century. Brahmin, from the name of the highest caste among the Hindus of India, stuck and is still very much in use today.[7]

HYSTERIA. This medical term (a functional disturbance of the nervous system, characterized by such disorders as convulsions) was first extended by American author, poet, editor, and literary critic **Edgar Allan Poe** (1809–1849) in 1839 to mean being in a morbidly excited condition; to express unhealthy emotions or excitement. The original medical term derives from a Latin term meaning womb because it was believed that the condition was more common in women.[8]

I

IDENTITY CRISIS. In psychology a period of uncertainty and confusion in which a person's sense of self becomes insecure, typically due to a change in his or her expected aims or role in society. Coined and defined by psychoanalyst-writer **Erik Erikson** (1902–1994) in his 1954 psychological profile of George Bernard Shaw.[1]

ILLTH. Antonym for wealth in the sense of well-being; ill-being. It was coined by British art critic and philanthropist **John Ruskin** (1819–1900) in 1862 in *Unto This Last*: "As mere accidental stays and impediments acting not as wealth, but (for we ought to have a correspondent term) as 'illth.'" He applied the term to designate those riches that appear to be desirable but are actually "fool's gold or worse."[2]

INCOMPOSSIBLE. Unable to exist if something else exists; not mutually possible. A term coined and defined by American author and satirist **Ambrose Bierce** (1842–1914) in his *Devil's Dictionary*.

INFANTICIPATE. Expecting a baby, a term created by the widely circulated American newspaper columnist **Walter Winchell** in 1934.

In Winchell's world, people didn't have babies. They "got storked," or had a "blessed event," or a "bundle from heaven." Winchell also takes credit for the state of expecting *infanticipation*. Winchell wrote the items for his newspaper columns and radio broadcasts in a brash style that influenced other writers. Divorce became *cancellation* or *Reno-vation*; bandleaders were *batoneers*; people in love were *cupiding*.[3]

INFRACANINOPHILE. One who habitually champions the underdog. The creation of American writer **Christopher Morley** (1890–1957).

INTERNATIONAL. The word *international* was coined by **Jeremy Bentham** (1748–1832) in the book *An Introduction to the Principles of Morals and Legislation* published in 1789. In the very first instance where the term appears, it is aligned with the word *jurisprudence*. *International jurisprudence* is suggested by the author to replace the term *law of nations*, what he deems to be "a misnomer."

IRON CURTAIN. The physical and symbolic wall that separated the West from the former Soviet Union and its satellite states. A term made famous by **Sir Winston Churchill** (1874–1965) on March 5, 1946, at Westminster College in the small Missouri town of Fulton in which he said, "From Stettin in the Baltic to Trieste in the Adriatic, an iron curtain has descended across the Continent." The phrase is often stated as having been coined by Churchill but recent evidence presented in *The Yale Book of Quotations* records that the English socialist and feminist **Ethel Snowden** (1880–1951) wrote in her 1920 book *Through Bolshevik Russia* that "we were behind the 'iron curtain' at last!" As the editor of *The Yale Book of Quotations*, Fred Shapiro pointed out "Snowden's meaning, referring to a barrier at the limit of Soviet influence, is the same as the Churchillian one." Britain's prime minister during the Second World War, in 1953 Churchill was the first world leader to be awarded the Nobel Prize in Literature. His writing included *A History of the English-Speaking Peoples*, a four-volume narrative and a six-volume history of the Second World War.[4]

IRREGULOUS. Defined by **Charles and Mary Cowden Clarke** in *The Shakespeare Key* in their list of **Shakespeare**an coinages that should be given wider currency. "Shakespeare invented the epithet 'irregulous' to express something much more strong than 'irregular'; something that combines the sense of 'disorderly,' 'lawless,' 'licentious,' as well as 'anomalous,' 'mongrel,' 'monstrous'—out of ordinary rule and order in every way." From *Cymbeline,* act 4, scene 2: "Conspir'd with that *irregulous* devil, Cloten."[5]

ISOLATOES. Term adopted from the Italian by American author **Herman Melville** (1819–1891) in his novel *Moby-Dick* to describe those spiritually isolated from their fellow man. "They were nearly all Islanders on the *Pequod, Isolatoes* too, I call such, not acknowledging the common continent of men, but each *Isolato* living on a separate continent of his own."

IT. An intangible quality of sexual attraction that a woman either had or lacked. The creation of novelist **Elinor Glyn** (1864-1943), the term was so commonly applied to Clara Bow that she was called "the *it* girl." One of Bow's movies was called simply *It*.

IVY LEAGUE. A group of eight universities in the northeastern United States that are regarded to be among the best in America. Coined by sportswriter **Caswell Adams** in 1937 as a term for the then-powerful eastern football league, it originally included Army and Navy as well. Brown, Columbia, Cornell, Dartmouth, Harvard, University of Pennsylvania, Princeton, and Yale are the colleges of the Ivy League.

J

JAZZ AGE. American novelist **F. Scott Fitzgerald** is recognized as the voice of the *Jazz Age*, a term he coined retrospectively in his 1931 essay "Echoes of the Jazz Age" to refer to the decade after World War I and before the stock market crash in 1929 during which Americans embarked upon what he called "the gaudiest spree in history." In the essay, Fitzgerald referred to "a whole race going hedonistic." *The Great Gatsby*, which echoes his relationship with his wife, Zelda Sayre, would go on to be considered one of the best American novels of all time.[1]

JEKYLL AND HYDE. Describing a person whose moral character and demeanor differs greatly from one situation to the next. It is one of the more powerful and lasting metaphoric references in literature borrowed directly from **Robert Lewis Stevenson**'s 1886 novella *Strange Case of Dr. Jekyll and Mr. Hyde*, in which a decent man, Jekyll, struggles with an evil alter ego, Hyde.

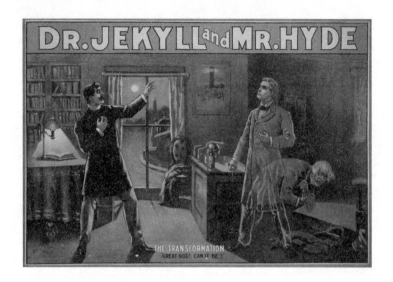

JOCK. Short for jockstrap, which appears in **Bernard Malamud**'s (1914–1986) *The Natural*: "He located his jock, with two red apples in it, swinging from a cord." It is later that the word becomes synonymous with school and college athletes. It is first reported in *American Speech* in 1963.[2]

JUNKY. Worthless. A **George Orwell**ian neologism of 1946 that appears in his *Collection of Essays* "The kind of junky books ... that accumulate in the bottoms of cupboards."

JUVESCENSE. The state of becoming young; the spring of the year. Created by American-born poet and publisher **T. S. Eliot** (1888–1965) in 1920 in the line from the poem "Gerontion": "In the juvescence of the year Came Christ the tiger." Anthony Burgess in a 1989 review of the second edition of the *Oxford English Dictionary* calls the term a solecism and writes of Eliot and the *OED:* "He was wrong; it should be 'juvenescence.' His authority prevails, and we can dishonor Latin etymology as we wish. The *OED* bestows the right."[3]

KELEMENOPY. Word created by poet **John Ciardi** (1916-1986) that appears in his *Browser's Dictionary*. It is "a sequential straight line through the middle of everything leading nowhere." It is based on the k-l-m-n-o-p sequence of the midalphabet.

KICKSHAW. Variously, a fancy dish, a trinket, a gewgaw, a trifle. In 2003 when the *Shakespeare Oxford Newsletter* published Michael Macrone's long list of terms coined by **Shakespeare**, a reader wrote a letter to complain of an omission that read in part: "The article only omits one favorite of mine, much in evidence at cocktail parties in the 1930s in the United Kingdom—'kickshaws'—now more often referred to, less attractively, as 'nibbles.' Some supposed it to be a leftover from the Indian Raj and it often came as a surprise that the word was first used by Shakespeare. This was in 1597 in 2 Henry IV v. 1, 'a joint of Mutton and any pretty little kickshawes,' meaning something elegant but insubstantial, from the French *quelquechose*. Shakespeare also uses the word in 12th

Night (1.3), not of nibbles, but of 'maskes etc.' 'Art thou good at these kicksechawses?' "[1]

KINSPIRIT. A fellow enthusiast; one impassioned with the same zeal or hobby or enthusiasm. It is the blend of *kindred* and *spirit* created by American journalist, novelist, essayist, and poet **Christopher Morley**: "We rather like the look of it; it has a droll, benign, elfish appearance as we put it down."

Morley worked to get wide acceptance for the word by periodically writing about it in his column for the *New York Evening Post*, but to little avail. More than twenty-five years after the coinage, Morley told the editor of *Word Study* that he had been able to "get it into small circulation here and there."[2]

KNOCK, KNOCK. WHO'S THERE? The knock-knock joke was, according to research conducted by poet and anthologist William Cole, a creation of a group of American writers led by humorist, poet, and wit **Dorothy Parker** (1893–1967) and followed by **Marc Connelly** and **Robert Benchley**, who were performing a *knock-knock* ritual as early as 1920 at the famous gathering at the Algonquin Hotel in New York known as the Algonquin Round Table. Cole came on this while reading Edmund Wilson's *The Twenties*, and he then got off a report published in the *New York Times* on October 20, 1982. Cole quoted Wilson's passage discussing (and generally dismissing) the Algonquin Round Table. He writes, "At one time their favorite game consisted of near-punning use of words. 'Have you heard Dotty's "Hiawatha" / "Hiawatha nice girl till I met you."' " A later entry in Wilson's diary discusses Parker, giving a couple of really bad knock-knocks, and this rather good one:

Knock, knock.
Who's there?
Scrantoknow.
Scrantoknow who?
Scrantoknow you're appreciated.

LACKLUSTER. Dull, mediocre, lacking brightness. A word that comes to us from **William Shakespeare**, who, as Jeffrey McQuain and Stanley Malless point out in *Coined by Shakespeare,* had a fondness for using *lack* in combinations such as *lack-beard, lack-brain, lack-linen,* and *lack-love* pointing out that lack is related to the Middle Dutch *lak* for deficiency. *Lackluster* makes its debut in *As You Like It,* in which Jaques describes the antics of a fool: "He drew a diall from his poake: And looking on it, with lacke-lustre eye . . ."[1]

LAME-BRAINED. A synonym for stupid, introduced by **P. G. Wodehouse** in 1929 in *Mr. Mulliner Speaking*: "A girl with an aunt who knew all about Shakespeare and Bacon must of necessity live in a mental atmosphere into which a lame-brained bird like himself could scarcely hope to soar." The term was turned into a noun for stupid person, a *lamebrain* as renamed by American humorist and screenwriter **S. J. Perelman** in 1945 in his book *Crazy Like a Fox* in which a female character is addressed as "Miss Lame Brain."

LAST HURRAH. A last campaign or valedictory act of a public figure or institution. The term comes from the title of American radio personality, journalist, and novelist **Edwin O'Connor**'s (1918–1968) 1956 novel *The Last Hurrah*, which was a fictionalized version of the life of **James Michael Curley** (1874–1958), mayor of Boston. A 1958 movie version starred Spencer Tracy and was directed by John Ford.

LILLIPUTIAN. Adjective used to describe something small or miniature. Created by **Jonathan Swift** in 1727 when he wrote *Gulliver's Travels*. He created the island of Lilliput in which the size of the inhabitants was no larger than the size of a human finger.

LINOTYPE. **Whitelaw Reid** (1837–1912), editor of the *New-York Tribune*, originated the name *linotype* for Ottmar Mergenthaler's invention when he examined a line-long slug and cried, "It's a line of type."[2]

LITTERBUG. Word coined by **Alice Rush McKeon** (1884–1979), a fierce and early advocate of highway beautification. Her 1931 book *The Litterbug Family* was instrumental in passing the first billboard control law in her home state of Maryland.[3]

LITTLE GREY CELLS. The neurons of the brain that allow fictional Belgian detective Hercule Poirot to click his heels and solve innumerable cases in English mystery author **Agatha Christie**'s (1890–1976) many stories about the fastidious detective. When asked by a reporter where she got the term, Christie replied, "I suppose I must have *invented* it. I suppose I must have."[4]

LIVING-ROOM WAR. Phrase coined by writer **Michael Arlen** (1895–1956) for an armed conflict that was played out on television. The Vietnam War later became the archetype.

LOST GENERATION. The period during which World War I was fought (1914–1918), when a high proportion of  young men were killed in the trenches; also used more generally of any generation judged to have been deprived of opportunities. The term was coined by **Gertrude Stein** (1874–1946) and made its debut in print in 1926 on the title page of Ernest Hemingway's *The Sun Also Rises:*

You are all a lost generation.

—Gertrude Stein in conversation

LOW MAN ON A TOTEM POLE. The least successful individual in a group; the person with the least status. Created by American humorist **H. Allen Smith** (1907–1976) as the title for his 1941 bestseller. The book sold over a million copies and was the first in a series of Smith books with memorable, offbeat titles—*Life in a Putty Knife Factory, Lost in the Horse Latitudes,* etc.

LOWBROW. See HIGHBROW/LOWBROW.

ℳ

MCJOB. Name for a low-pay, low-prestige, low-benefit, no-future job in the service sector, based on the proclivity of the McDonald's food chain to preface the names of their products with the proprietary *Mc* prefix, such as Chicken McNuggets. The term was coined by sociologist **Amitai Etzioni** and made its debut in print in the *Washington Post* on August 24, 1986, in the article "The Fast-Food Factories: McJobs Are Bad for Kids" and then popularized by Canadian writer **Douglas Coupland** in his novel *Generation X: Tales for an Accelerated Culture.*

MALAGA. A curse. In his *The Vicomte de Bragelonne*, **Alexandre Dumas** has his character Planchet invent a swear word to be employed only in the direst circumstances: "Malaga!" For its intended purpose it achieved some good reviews. Alfred George Gardiner, the essayist, commented, "It is a good swearword. It has the advantage of meaning nothing, and that is precisely what a swearword should mean. It should be sound and fury, signifying nothing. It should be incoherent, irrational, a little crazy like the passion which evokes it."

MALAPROP. An incorrect word in place of a word with a similar sound, resulting in a nonsensical, often humorous utterance. This eponym word originated from the character Mrs. Malaprop, in the 1775 play *The Rivals* by Irish playwright, poet, and long-term owner of London's Theatre Royal, Drury Lane, **Richard Brinsley Sheridan** (1751–1816). As you might expect, Mrs. Malaprop is full of amusing mistakes, exclaiming, "He's the very pineapple of success!" and "She's as headstrong as an allegory on the banks of the Nile!" The adjective *malaproprian* is first used, according to the *OED*, by George Eliot. "Mr. Lewes is sending what a Malapropian friend once called a 'missile' to Sara."[1]

MALTREATER. Word that debuts in American writer **Owen Wister**'s (1860–1938) *The Virginian* in 1902: "A maltreater of hawses [horses.]" Wister is regarded as the "father" of Western fiction, who helped establish the cowboy as an American folk hero and stock fictional character.

MASTER OF THE UNIVERSE. Someone in absolute control, a term created by **John Dryden** in his 1690 play *Amphitryon*: "I'm all on fire; and would not loose this Night, To be the Master of the Universe." In 1982 the term was patented in the plural as the name of a series of toy action figures with names like He-Man and Skeletor. In 1987, novelist **Tom Wolfe** recoined the term, alluding to the action figures, as a person who is exceptionally successful in the world of high finance in his novel *The Bonfire of the Vanities*.

MATA HARI. A beautiful and seductive female spy; by extension a *femme fatale*. Created by English writer of novels, biogra-

phies, and travel books **Evelyn Waugh** (1903–1966) after Margaretha Geertruida "M'greet" Zelle MacLeod, better known by the stage name Mata Hari. She was a Dutch exotic dancer and accused spy who was executed by firing squad in France under charges of espionage for Germany during World War I. The stage name came from the Malay word *mata* for eye and *hari* for day, which as a compound means sun. Waugh turned it into an eponym in 1936 in *Waugh in Abyssinia*: "Patrick's spy ... was soon known to the European community as Mata Hari." In the 1967 movie version of Ian Fleming's *Casino Royale*, James Bond has conceived a daughter, Mata Bond, with Hari. This would have been impossible since the daughter's fictional birth was three years after the real female spy died.

MAU-MAU. To terrorize by intimidation, a creation of Tom Wolfe in his 1970 work *Radical Chic and Mau-Mauing Flak*

Catchers. "Going downtown to mau-mau the bureaucrats got to be the routine practice in San Francisco." The name came from the Mau Mau, an anti-European secret society in colonial Kenya.

ME DECADE. Label for the 1970s in America that was coined by novelist **Tom Wolfe** in *New York* magazine in August 1976, describing the new preoccupation with self-awareness and the collective retreat from history, community, and human reciprocity.[2]

MEEKER. To visit places that have acquired some sort of shrine status. As demonstrated by its inventor, **Ivor Brown**, "Myriads ... go meekering at Stratford-upon-Avon."

MELTING POT. Metaphor for a unified albeit diverse United States, first employed in this sense of the term by writer **Israel Zangwill** (1864–1926) in his 1908 play *The Melting Pot*, which developed the theme. The term was enthusiastically embraced by turn-of-the-century Americans who were eager to find a unifying national concept at a time when the United States was becoming more ethnically diverse than ever before. "The metaphor was hugely popular when it was introduced, and the play was a big success with the general public," wrote Peter D. Salins in his book *Assimilation, American Style.* He added, "President Theodore Roosevelt was so enamored of the play's message that he compared Zangwill favorably to George Bernard Shaw and Henrik Ibsen. Popular faith in the melting pot survived both the

Great Depression and World War II. But it did not survive the 1960s."[3]

While Zangwill made the term popular it was created in a different context by essayist, lecturer, and poet **Ralph Waldo Emerson** (1803–1882), who heralded this philosophy in 1845 when he wrote in his journal "so in this continent—asylum of all nations,—the energy of the Irish, Germans, Swedes, Poles, and Cossacks, and all the European tribes—of the Africans, and of the Polynesians, will construct a new race, a new religion, a new state, a new literature, which will be as vigorous as the new Europe which came out of the melting pot of the Dark Ages."

MEME. The fundamental units of culture, like DNA. First coined in 1976 by the evolutionary biologist **Richard Dawkins**, "a meme represents ideas, behaviors or styles that spread from person to person. It can be a trendy dance, a viral video, a new fashion, a technological tool or a catchphrase. Like viruses, memes arise, spread, mutate and die." One of the problems with the term that may hamper its ultimate use in conversational English is that there is considerable confusion as to how to pronounce the word.

MENTAL MASTURBATION. A vivid metaphor constructed by **Lord Byron** (1788-1824) and applied to John Keats. In a letter to his publisher, John Murray, he said of the poet: "Such writing is a sort of mental masturbation—he is always frigging his imagination—I don't mean that he is indecent but viciously soliciting his own ideas into a state which is

neither poetry nor anything else but a Bedlam of vision produced by raw pork and opium."[4]

MICROCOMPUTER. A small computer employing micro-
processors based on a single chip. In the July 1956 issue of the
Magazine of Fantasy & Science Fiction American science fiction
writer **Isaac Asimov** (1920–1992) debuted the term in a story
called "The Dying Night" in this line: "It had become the hall-
mark of the scientist, much as ... the microcomputer that of
the statistician." The term is often paired with the word *revolution* to describe the period beginning in the early 1980s when
inexpensive personal computers first became available to the
public. Asimov was a prolific writer who was the first (and,
thus far, only) author to have a book in every one of the ten
categories in the Dewey decimal classification (generalities,
philosophy, religion, social sciences, language, natural sciences,
technology, the arts, literature, and lastly geography and
history).

MIDDLE AMERICA. Journalist **Joseph Kraft** (1924–
1986) of the *Washington Post* is credited with inventing the
term. Kraft also served as a speech writer for John F.
Kennedy.[5]

MILQUETOAST. A painfully timid and ineffectual male—
or in British terms a milksop. An eponym inspired by cartoonist **H. T. Webster**'s (1885–1952) character Caspar
Milquetoast in his 1924 *Timid Soul* cartoon strip and named
after a once-popular American dish, *milk toast,* which during
the nineteenth and early twentieth centuries was thought to

be a proper and soothing dish for ill children and the ailing aged.[*]

M I L V E R. A person with a strong interest in common with another, but especially an interest in words and wordplay. Coined by American essayist and critic **Logan Pearsall Smith** (1865–1946) in response to a friend's lament that there was no satisfactory word in English for "a person who is enthusiastic about the same thing you are enthusiastic about." Smith decided it was too clumsy to say fellow fan or coenthusiast; so he created the word *milver*, which had the added advantage of giving poets a word they could rhyme with *silver*. As he explained in his 1936 book *Reperusals and Recollections*, "Language being never adequate to describe all the relationships of people to each other, I have invented the word *milver* to describe those who share a fad in common." There is a myth that no English word rhymes with silver, but there are several existing words to which milver is added. The others are *chilver*, *filver*, and *hilver*. Chilver is an Old English noun meaning a ewe lamb.

---

[*] When the author of this book, born in 1939, was young and under the weather he was served milk toast from a recipe of his grandmother's that probably came from her kitchen bible Fannie Merritt Farmer's *The Boston Cooking-School Cook Book*. (Boston: Little, Brown, 1918).

Here is the recipe for Milk Toast from that book:

1 pint scalded milk
½ teaspoon salt
2 tablespoons butter
4 tablespoons cold water
2½ tablespoons bread flour
6 slices dry toast

Add cold water gradually to flour to make a smooth, thin paste. Add to milk, stirring constantly until thickened, cover, and cook twenty minutes; then add salt and butter in small pieces. Dip slices of toast separately in sauce; when soft, remove to serving dish. Pour remaining sauce over all.

MITTY. See WALTER MITTY.

MOANISM. Habitual lamenting, the creation of poet **Robert Frost**, and now regarded as a Frostian nonce word.[6]

MOBY DICK. Something important, impressive, and by extension rare or even unique. Likened to the great white whale central to **Herman Melville**'s novel of the same name, Melville appears to have adopted the name from real-life albino sperm whale, known as Mocha Dick that lived near the island of Mocha off Chile's southern coast, several decades before he wrote his book.[*]

MODERNISM. Characteristic of modern times or something with distinctly modern features. The term first appeared in 1737 as an apparent coinage of **Jonathan Swift** in a letter to Alexander Pope decrying the "corruption of English by those Scribblers who send us over their trash in Prose and Verse, with abominable curtailing and quaint modernisms."[7] See also POSTMODERNISM.

MODUS VIVENDI. A Latin phrase (way of living) referring to a practical compromise; especially one that bypasses

---

[*] It is a name that has an odd unexplained appeal to those who name commercial ventures, especially restaurants. Within ten miles of the author's house there is an Afghan takeout, a kebob restaurant, and a sushi restaurant all named Moby-Dick. Also, the name of Captain Ahab's first mate in the novel is a Quaker seaman from Nantucket named Starbuck, which was adopted as the name for the Starbucks international chain of coffee shops. Owner of the chain, Howard Schultz, noted in his 2011 book *Pour Your Heart Into It* that [Starbucks cofounder Gordon] Bowker and other investors discussed naming the company Pequod after the ship in *Moby-Dick*. Then they decided no one would want to drink a cup of "Pee-quod." (http://blog.seattlepi .com/thebigblog/2012/06/29/how-starbucks-got-its-name/)

difficulties and is resolved peacefully. First written in English by American writer **Henry James** (1843–1916) in the *Nation* magazine in 1875 discussing the Jews: "In Portugal they found a modus Vivendi which, though still hard, was easier than the Spanish rule."

MOLE. A high-level penetration agent who betrays his or her intelligence service sharing its secrets with its enemy; and by extension any informant buried within an organization. The term was popularized by British spy novelist **John le Carré** in 1974 in his novel *Tinker, Tailor, Soldier, Spy,* where many believed it made its debut: "Ivlov's task was to service a mole. A mole is a deep penetration agent so called because he burrows deep into the fabric of Western imperialism." Le Carré never claimed to have coined the term, only to have revived the term. According to Joseph C. Goulden in his *Dictionary of Espionage,* Walter Pforzheimer, former CIA legislative counsel, states that the term was actually first used by British philosopher, statesman, and author **Sir Francis Bacon** in his 1622 biography of King Henry VII: "He was careful and liberal to obtain good Intelligence from all parts abroad . . . He had such Moles perpetually working and casting to undermine him." The *OED,* which does not list the Bacon reference, lists several twentieth-century earlier uses including a 1964 book by Geoffrey Bailey on Russian intelligence called *The Conspirators* that reported that in 1935 the Russians recruited a Captain Fedosenko as a double agent and gave him the alias "The Mole." That said it was le Carré[8] who made the term a key one in both reality and fiction in the decades following publication of the novel.

MOMISM. Term for excessive attachment to one's mother, created by science fiction writer and self-appointed social critic **Philip Wylie** (1902–1971) in an essay in his 1942 *Generation of Vipers*. Wylie's contention was that mothers had turned their children, but mostly their sons, into resourceless, eternally dependent fools. "Mom," he wrote, "is a middle-aged puffin with an eye like a hawk that has just seen a rabbit twitch far below. She is about twenty-five pounds overweight, with no sprint, but sharp heels and a hard backhand which she does not regard as a foul but a womanly defense. In a thousand of her there is not sex appeal enough to budge a hermit ten paces off a rock ledge." Wylie's mindless venom and the issue of *momism* created a national controversy for more than a decade. His most quoted line on the subject: "She is the corpse at every wedding and the bride at every funeral."

MONDEGREEN. A term for misheard song lyrics, coined by American freelance writer **Sylvia Wright** (1920–1961) in 1954. It derived from her long-held belief that a song contained the line, "They had slain the Earl of Moray and Lady Mondegreen." In fact, the line ended with the words, "and laid him on the green." There have been a number of books, articles, and Internet sites devoted to collecting such classic examples as "Deck the Halls with Buddy Holly," "He's Got the Whole World in His Pants," and the Elton John classic, "Ken Doll in the Wind." In a series of articles on *mondegreens* in the *Minneapolis Star Tribune*, writer Dave Matheny gave a number of fine examples including the hymn "Lead on, O King Eternal," which became "Lead on, O Kinky Turtle."

MONKEY TRIAL. Term first coined by **H. L. Mencken** himself for the 1925 Scopes trial, the first American "trial of the century," which pitted the modernist against the fundamentalist and the provincial in a courtroom drama of enormous interest, much of it engineered by Mencken. Forty years later, Scopes would say, "In a way, it was Mencken's show."

MONOLOGOPHOBE. Creation of American journalist and editor **Theodore M. Bernstein** (1904–1979), who defined this creature in his 1965 writer's handbook *The Careful Writer* as "a writer who would rather walk naked in front of Saks Fifth Avenue than be caught using the same word more than once in three lines." See also SYNONYMOMANIA.

MORON. A word created by eugenicist **H. H. Goddard** (1866-1957), director of research at the Vineland Training School for Feebleminded Boys and Girls in New Jersey. In a 1910 journal article, Goddard gave a stunningly broad definition of moron as one who is lacking in intelligence, one who is deficient in judgment or sense. To Goddard, alcoholics, criminals, prostitutes, unemployed, and people who acted immorally in general were obviously lacking intelligence, judgment, or sense, and were, therefore, morons. Those involved in the eugenics movement believed that the human species could be improved by selective breeding—encouraging those from a superior gene pool and discouraging the inferior members of society including morons. The term is now considered offensive, and along with *imbecile* and *idiot*, these terms have been abolished in clinical practice.[9]

MOTEL. A roadside hotel designed for motorists with easy access from one's parked car. A blend of *motor* and *hotel,* it was coined by architect **Arthur S. Heineman** (1878–1972), who copyrighted the term after opening the first one in 1925 in San Luis Obispo, halfway between San Francisco and Los Angeles. For $1.25 a night, guests were issued a two-room bungalow with a kitchen and a private adjoining garage.

MUCH ADO ABOUT NOTHING. A great deal of fuss over something of no importance. The phrase is the title of **Shakespeare**'s comedic play of the same name written about 1588–1599. He had used the word *ado*, which means business or activity, in an earlier play —*Romeo and Juliet,* "Weele keepe no great adoe, a Friend or two."

MUDHOOK. An anchor in early American slang that makes its debut in print in **James Fenimore Cooper**'s 1827 great novel of the sea, *The Red Rover:* "He would fasten her to the spot with good hempen cables and iron mud-hooks."

MUDSCAPE. A landscape composed largely or entirely of mud. A creation of **O. Henry** in 1908 in the "Gentle Grafter": "The third day of the rain it slacked up awhile in the afternoon, so me and Andy walked out to the edge of town to view the mudscape."

MUGGLE. A person with no magical powers and by extension anyone regarded inferior, especially in the workplace in the realm of the Harry Potter novels by **J. K. Rowling**. The *OED* says she first mentioned *muggles* in 1997 in *Harry Potter* *and the Philosopher's Stone:* "Rejoice, for You-Know-Who has gone at last! Even Muggles like yourself should be celebrating this happy, happy day!"[*][10]

Rowling has been titled the world's first billion-dollar author, having earned that amount from her Harry Potter books. She is also, according to *Forbes* magazine, one of only five self-made female billionaires up to 2004 when she hit the billion-dollar mark.[11]

MUGWUMPS. *New York Sun* editor **Charles Dana** (1819–1897) created this term to describe those who desert their political party to support another candidate, particularly the Republicans who would not support the candidacy of James G. Blaine, the Republican candidate for president in 1884.

MUNCHKIN. A minor player; derogatory term for someone who is unimportant though often endearing. Alluding to the diminutive creatures in *The Wonderful Wizard of Oz* created by **L. Frank Baum** (1856–1919) in both his 1900 book and the 1939 motion picture in which the Munchkins help Dorothy in her quest for the city of Oz. According to the *Collins English Dictionary*, Munchkin is also a breed of medium-sized cat with short legs.

---

[*] According to Arthur Waldhorn's *Concise Dictionary of the American Language* (p. 111) and other sources, *muggles* is a "narcotic addict's term for marijuana." The *OED* lists a number of additional senses for this word (resembling a fishtail; a young woman, etc.) spanning from the thirteenth to the twentieth centuries. Anu Garg discussed the many meanings of muggle in a 2013 entry in his *A Word a Day* Internet service: "And that's how a language grows. Old words die—or take on a new life. New words appear. Language wordstock is replenished, refreshed, and the language remains vibrant and serviceable, ready to describe new concepts, ideas, and objects."

MURDERMONGRESS. A female writer of murder stories, a term invented by **Ogden Nash** to describe Agatha Christie in his 1957 anthology *You Can't Get There from Here.* The word was fashioned to rhyme with Library of Congress.

MUSCLEMAN. **James Fenimore Cooper**'s term for a man of superior strength. As he first used it in 1838 in *Homeward Bound*: "I suppose these muscle men will not have much use for any but the oyster-knives, as I am informed they eat with their fingers." According to the *OED*, the use of the term to mean a man who uses force to get his way does not come into the language until 1929.[12]

MUTT AND JEFF. Two people with widely divergent characteristics in the manner of the mismatched comic strip pair extended to a lowercase metaphor by American poet **E. E. Cummings** (1894–1962) in 1917 when he wrote: "By failing to get up ... I escaped departing with the bums mutts and jeffs (not  to say ginks, slobs, and punks) who came over with us."[13]

NADSAT. Name for the dialectical (and diabolical) slang created by British writer **Anthony Burgess** (1917–1993) for his violent gang characters, Alex and his *droogs* (pals), in his 1962 novel *A Clockwork Orange*. Like many lexical items in the novel, this word derives from transliterated or anglicized Russian, along with *baboochka* (old woman), *bezoomny* (mad), *bitva* (battle), *gulliver* (head), *horrorshow* (good), *koshka* (cat), *krovvy* (blood), *malchick* (boy), *skazzed* (said), *voloss* (hair), and many others. Nadsat also includes some Cockney-derived words and other inventions: *viddy* (see), *pretty polly* (money), *platties* (clothes), and so on. A Cockney expression, "as queer as a clockwork orange" means "very queer indeed," with or without a sexual implication.[1]

NASALISM. Nasal pronunciation. A term created and applied to the modern American voice by **Oscar Wilde**, who never got to hear Bob Dylan to whom the term was later applied. Wilde introduced the term in the sentence: "The nasalism of the modern American had been retained from the Puritan Fathers."[2]

NATURE DEFICIT DISORDER. Author and child advocacy expert **Richard Louv** coined the term to describe modern children growing up without contact with the natural world. In his 2005 book *Last Child in the Woods: Saving Our Children from Nature-Deficit Disorder*, Louv links the lack of nature in children's lives to depression, obesity, attention deficit disorder, anxiety, and stress. The term aptly applies to adults, individuals, families, and communities many times over.

NEOPHILIAC. A lover of the new, a pejorative term created in 1970 by **Christopher Booker**, British writer and editor of the satirical magazine *Private Eye*. His book *The Neophiliacs* had a sharp edge and his thesis was that when a society is in a state of disintegration and flux, its members opt for false revolutions in style and manner over genuine self-renewal. The dream of a new "fun" England had, in Booker's view, darkened into a nightmare of drugs, depravity, and anger. Critic Melvin Maddocks, reviewing the book for the *Christian Science Monitor*, summed it up this way: "The Neophiliacs have granted themselves a doubtful gift of freedom without a sense of purpose. They are free to Do Their Thing—if only they could remember what it is they thought they wanted to do."

NERD. The word first appears in print in 1950 in the children's book *If I Ran the Zoo* by American children's writer **Dr. Seuss** (Theodor Seuss Geisel

1904–1991). In the book a boy named Gerald McGrew makes a great number of delightfully extravagant claims as to what he would do if he were in charge at the zoo where, he insists, the animals housed there were boring. Among these fanciful schemes is:

And then just to show them, I'll sail to Ka-Troo
And bring back an IT-KUTCH, a PREEP, and a
    PROO,
A NERKLE, a NERD, and SEERSUCKER, too!

The accompanying illustration for *nerd* shows a grumpy Seuss creature with unruly hair and sideburns, wearing a black T-shirt—not terribly nerdlike. For whatever reasons, *it-kutch, preep, proo,* and *nerkle* have never been enshrined in any dictionary.

NESOMANIAC. A person who is mad about islands. A creation of American author **James A. Michener** (1907–1997), who introduced it in the January 1978 issue of *Travel and Leisure*.

NEWSPEAK. Artificial language spoken in **George Orwell**'s dystopic *1984*. An example of this language is the word *Duckspeak*, which is a *Newspeak* term meaning literally to quack like a duck or to speak without thinking. Duckspeak can be either good or *ungood* (bad), depending on who is speaking, and whether what they are saying is in following with the ideals of Big Brother. To speak rubbish and lies may be ungood, but to speak rubbish and lies for the good of "The Party" may be good. *Oldspeak* refers to conventional English, which would have been superseded by Newspeak by the year 2050.

NIBFUL. A literary measure created and used by English author **Virginia Woolf** (1882–1941). As much ink as a nib can hold; also a small amount of writing in 1930 in her *Diaries*: "I have just finished, with this very nib-ful of ink, the last sentence of *The Waves*."

NINJA. One trained in the feudal Japanese art of ninjutsu and/or specially trained for assassination and espionage. Term and concept introduced into English by British spy novelist **Ian Fleming** in 1964 in the James Bond novel *You Only Live Twice*: "The men ... are now learning to be *ninja* or 'stealers-in.'" It was popularized by such works as Eric Van Lustbader's 1980 novel *The Ninja* and the 1981 film *Enter the Ninja*.

The term has proliferated to the point that a 2013 Google search for the word yielded 427 million hits. There is a site online, for instance, called Ninjawords, which according to its home page, is "optimized to return a definition instantly as soon as you hit enter, and your search is spellchecked in multiple ways until we find a good match. Ninjas like to stay lean and mean, which is why there is no junk cluttering your dictionary, slowing you down."[3]

NO-NECK. Pejorative noun or adjective for a person with a short neck or large head who by extension is to be shunned. It appears to have been coined as an insult in American playwright **Tennessee Williams**'s (1911–1983) 1955 play *Cat on a Hot Tin Roof:* "One of those no-neck monsters hit me with some ice cream." Maggie says of the children in the house: "Their fat little heads sit on their fat little bodies without a bit of connection . . . you can't wring their necks if they got no necks to wring."

NON-ISM. The practice of prefacing a word with *non*—perhaps the ultimate example of a nonce word created by **James Thurber** in the December 1961 *Harper's* magazine. "There is non-fiction and non non-fiction . . . Speaking of nonism: the other day . . . the *Paris Herald Tribune* wrote, 'The non-violence became noisier.'" Non-ism is also used to mean a non-ideology. Although Thurber did not hyphenate the term, it has passed into wider use with a hyphen.

NYMPHET. Coined by Russian American novelist **Vladimir Nabokov** (1899–1977) for his novel *Lolita:* "Now I wish to introduce the following idea. Between the age limits of nine and fourteen there occur maidens who, to certain bewitched travelers, twice or many times older than they, reveal their true nature which is not human, but nymphic (that is, demoniac); and these chosen creatures I propose to designate as 'nymphets.' "

NYMPHOMANIACAL. Of excessive sexual desire in and behavior by a female. The noun was turned into play as an adjective by **Aldous Huxley** in his 1923 novel *Antic Hay:* "When I call my lover a nymphomaniacal dog, she runs the penknife into my arm."

ODYSSEY. A long and eventful or adventurous journey or experience. An allusion to **Homer**'s epic poem describing the travels of Odysseus during his ten years of wandering after the sack of Troy. He eventually returned home to Ithaca and killed the suitors who had plagued his wife, Penelope, during his absence. Homer was the first writer to dabble in epic poetry for which there is a written record.

OMBIBULOUS. H. L. Mencken's word for someone who drinks everything. "I am ombibulous." Mencken wrote of himself, "I drink every known alcoholic drink and enjoy them all."

ONE FELL SWOOP. It appears in **Shakespeare**'s *Macbeth*: "What! all my pretty chickens and their dame / At one fell swoop?" laments Macduff in act 4, scene 3, upon learning his wife and children have been killed by Macbeth. This appears to be the earliest recorded use of the phrase, although it may have been in common usage before Shakespeare wrote it down.

Michael Quinion, on his website World Wide Words, notes that an audience in Shakespeare's day would have immediately pictured "a falcon plummeting out of the sky to snatch its prey."

ONE UP/ONE-UPMANSHIP. See GAMESMANSHIP.

OXBRIDGE. Originally a fictional university introduced in British novelist **William Makepeace Thackery**'s novel *Pendennis*: "'Rough and ready, your chum seems,' the Major said. 'Somewhat different from your dandy friends at Oxbridge.'" Later it was taken as a composite for Oxford and Cambridge as a way of distinguishing those two universities from other British universities.[1]

OZ. A fictional city and land in the 1900 children's fantasy *The Wonderful Wizard of Oz*, by **L. Frank Baum**. Later, and most notably after the 1939 film version of the book, it referred to any place thought to resemble the land or city of Oz, especially any fantastic, ideal, or imaginary domain. The *OED* credits American writer Hart Crane as the first to extend the application of the name to a domain other than Baum's original. "It [*sc*. Tepoztlán, Mexico] was truly the Land of Oz, with the high valley walls in the Wizard's circle."

Oz is also slang for Australia. This is not only because of the allusion to the book and movie but because when Australia is referred to informally with its first three letters it becomes Aus. When Aus or Aussie, the short form for an Australian, is pronounced for fun with a hissing sound at the end, it sounds like the spelling Oz.[2]

p

PAGE 99 TEST. English novelist, poet, critic, and editor **Ford Madox Ford** (1873–1939) often recommended that readers not judge a book by its beginning pages. Instead he advised that readers "open the book to page ninety-nine and the quality of the whole will be revealed to you." The idea has been carried forth in the website Page99Test.com, which offers (courageous) authors and aspiring authors the chance to upload the ninety-ninth pages of their works and invite readers to comment on whether they would buy, or like to read, the rest.

PANDEMONIUM. For book 1 of his epic poem *Paradise Lost*, published in 1667, **John Milton** invented *Pandemonium*—from the Greek *pan* (all), and *daimon* (evil spirit), literally "a place for all the demons"—or as Milton first expressed in the poem: "A solemn Councel forthwith to be held At Pandæmonium, the high Capital Of Satan and his Peers." Later in the work he calls it the "citie and proud seat of Lucifer." By the end of the century, Pandemonium had become a synonym not just for hell, but, because the devils created a lot of noise, the meaning of *pandemonium,* now lowercased, was broadened to mean "uproar and tumult." In 1828 Edward Bulwer-Lytton applied it to a common location: "We found ourselves in that dreary pandaemonium . . . a Gin-shop." Today the term is applied to any scene of disarray, confusion, or even heightened activity as in the headline: IPAD PANDEMONIUM.[1]

PATHOGRAPHY. Term re-created by American author **Joyce Carol Oates** for any biography dwelling on the negative aspects of the life of the person being written about.[*] She contrasted it to the traditional biography in a *New York Times* book review of August 28, 1988: "A pathography typically focuses upon a far smaller canvas, sets its standards much lower. Its motifs are dysfunction and disaster, illnesses and pratfalls, failed marriages and failed careers, alcoholism and breakdowns and outrageous conduct." In his book on style *Spunk and Bite: A Writer's Guide to Bold, Contemporary Style,* Arthur Plotnik terms this coinage "that happy click when language perfectly fits the idea."

PEDESTRIAN. No one had an English word for someone who goes about on foot until 1791, when English Romantic poet **William Wordsworth** (1770–1850) coined the noun.

PERIPLUM. Coined by American poet **Ezra Pound** (1885–1972) to describe a tour that takes you round, then back again.

---

[*] The word was coined earlier for the biography of an illness—a true pathology. Oates never claimed to have coined the word—just that she gave it a secondary meaning.

PHEDINKUS. A nonsense word created by American newspaperman and author **Damon Runyon** (1880–1946) in 1935. It has survived largely because of its appeal to other writers. In his 1951 *I Break My Word*, Ivor Brown expressed his admiration for "the old phedinkus," noting that it had a "Grecian savour." In the introduction to *Guys and Dolls and Other Writings*, an anthology of Runyon's writing, Pete Hamill wrote: "Nobody alive knows what a 'phedinkus' is, and Runyon's stories are sprinkled with other words whose meanings have vanished into air. But their meanings can almost always be deciphered from context."

PHILATELY. This term for stamp collecting was coined by French stamp collector **Georges Herpin** in an 1864 article which appeared in the book *Le collectionneur de timbres-poste* (The collection of postage stamps). Herpin fashioned it from *phile-* (loving) and *ateleia* (exemption from tax). The tax reference dates to ancient Greek where the original function of postage stamps was to indicate that the cost of delivery had been prepaid by the sender. In H. W. Fowler's original *Modern English Usage* it is suggested that *philately* be avoided in favor of stamp collecting and stamp collector, adding, "It is a pity that for one of the most popular scientific pursuits one of the least popularly intelligible names should have been found."[2]

PHYSICIST. See SCIENTIST.

PICKSOME. Given to picking and choosing; selective. **Ivor Brown** coined it in his 1948 work *No Idle Words*: "The former is fastidious, and to be thus selective, thus picksome, is surely a virtue."

PLATONIC. Describing a relationship that is intimate and affectionate but not sexual; spiritual rather than physical. The term originally was associated with Plato before English poet and playwright **Ben Jonson** (1572–1637) gave it new meaning in 1631.[3]

PLENTIETH. **Franklin P. Adams**'s adjective of indefinite older age, as in: "He is about to celebrate his plentieth birthday."

PLOBBY. A word created by English humorist **P. G. Wodehouse** to describe the noise of a pig eating. He actually used it in conjunction with another word of his own invention to marvelous net effect: it was a "plobby, wofflesome sound."

PLUTOGRAPHY. **Tom Wolfe** coined the term for the graphic depiction of the lives of the rich especially as a genre of popular literature, journalism, and broadcasting. *Money* magazine quoted Wolfe: "Social observer Tom Wolfe calls the 80's the age of plutography, when a reverence for riches prevails."

POCKETA-POCKETA. **James Thurber**'s imitative construction for the sound of an internal combustion engine. "The pounding of the cylinders increased: ta-pocketa-pocketa-pocketa-pocketa-pocketa" is how he introduced the sound in the March 28, 1939, issue of the *New Yorker*.

PODSNAPPERY. The smugness of Mr. Podsnap in **Charles Dickens**'s *Our Mutual Friend* gave rise to this noun meaning a state of extreme self-satisfaction; a self-satisfied Philistine. Dickens is responsible for some of the most inventive character names in literature, including the Fezziwigs, the Jellybys, the Pardiggles, Chevy Slyme, Mrs. Spottletoe, Nicholas Tulrumble, and Wopsle. Dickens is the master of the *charactronym*—the name of a literary character that is especially suited to his or her personality. Lexicographer Richard Lederer wrote: "The enormous and enduring popularity of Charles Dickens's works springs in part from the writer's skill at creating memorable charactronyms—Scrooge, the tightfisted miser; Mr. Gradgrind, the tyrannical schoolmaster; Jaggers, the rough-edged lawyer; and Miss Havisham ('have a sham'), the jilted spinster who lives in an illusion."

POLLYANNA. To be naïvely cheerful and optimistic; unrealistically happy. From the name of the fictional character created by **Eleanor Hodgman Porter** (1868–1920), American children's author. It first appears in her 1913 work *Pollyanna:* "'Her name is Pollyanna Whittier' . . . 'And what are the special ingredients of this wonder-working—tonic of hers?' . . . 'As near as I can find out it is an overwhelming, unquenchable gladness . . . Her quaint speeches are constantly being repeated to me, and, as near as I can make out, just being glad is the tenor of most of them."[4]

POLYPHILOPROGENITIVE. Very prolific or fecund, a word coined by **T. S. Eliot** in 1919 and employed in a poem entitled "Mr. Eliot's Sunday Morning Service."

POOH STICKS. A game in which sticks are thrown into a river from the upstream side of a bridge, the winner being the person whose stick emerges first on the other side. Created by **A. A. Milne** and introduced in 1928 in *The House at Pooh Corner*. The game has long been played by humans and even has a rule book, *The Official Pooh Corner Rules for Playing Poohsticks*, which was written in 1996 to commemorate the seventieth anniversary of the publication of *Winnie-the-Pooh*. The annual World Pooh Sticks Championship held at Day's Lock, Little Wittenham, had to be canceled in 2013 because the river was too high.

POOSE. Poet **Alastair Reid**'s word for a drop that hangs on the end of the nose and glistens. A poose is likely to appear when one has a cold or comes out of the water after swimming.

PORTMANTEAU WORD. Term coined by **Lewis Carroll** for merging two existing words into one new word, e.g., his words *slithy* from *lithe + slimy* and *chortle* from *chuckle + snort*. In such blending, parts of two familiar words are yoked together (usually the first part of one word and the second part of the other) to produce a word that conveys the meanings and sound of the old ones—*smog* from *smoke + fog*, *motel* from *motor + hotel*, *heliport* from *helicopter + airport*, and *brunch* from *breakfast + lunch*. *Portmanteau* itself is a quaint word for *suitcase*, originally combining *porter* (to carry) and *manteau* (cloak) to make a name for a cloak-transporting suitcase designed for carrying on horseback. Lexicographer Ben Zimmer has noted that the portmanteau "remains perhaps the most popular method of new word formation in English, from slang ('chillax,' 'geektastic') to business jargon ('webinar,' 'advertorial')."[5]

POSSLQ. Acronym for either "person of opposite sex sharing living quarters or partner of opposite sex sharing living quarters"—in other words a person of the opposite sex living at the same address as another, specifically one who is a sexual partner but not a spouse. In early references this was reported as an official US Census Bureau demographic classification; but while it was never adopted by the government, it attained wide popular use. The term was coined by **Arthur J. Norton**, a member of the US Census Bureau, but given a great lift by radio commentator and broadcast poet **Charles Osgood** in his poem "My POSSLQ," which opened with the stanza:

> Come live with me and be my love,
> And we will some new pleasures prove
> Of golden sands and crystal brooks
> With silken lines, and silver hooks.
> There's nothing that I wouldn't do
> If you would be my POSSLQ.[*]

POSTMODERNISM. The term *postmodern* was coined in the late 1940s by British historian **Arnold Toynbee** (1889–1975) in his monumental multivolume *A Study of History*. Toynbee was convinced that a new historical epoch had begun, in the post–World War I era with the emergence of "mass society," where the normal working class played a more important

---

[*] The first line of this poem is taken from the first line of John Donne's "The Bait."

role than the capitalist class. The term was redeployed in the mid-1970s by the American art critic and theorist Charles Jencks to describe contemporary antimodernist movements like pop art.[*]

POWER ELITE. American sociologist **C. Wright Mills** (1916–1962) created the term in a 1956 book of the same title to characterize a new coalition of three ruling groups that rose to dominance in the post–World War II United States that composed the power elite: the military, large corporations, and government leaders. He thought this concentration of power was progressively more centralized and undemocratic. *The Power Elite* was one of a series of books that came about within a few years of one another and leveled a critical eye at America. Each book had a title that entered the language as metaphor: *The Lonely Crowd* by David Riesman and Nathan Glazer described the changing and increasingly conformist and "other-directed" American character; *The Organization Man* by William H. Whyte looked at the corporate executive and the movement of business leadership from rugged individualism to collectivist thinking; *The Hidden Persuaders* by Vance Packard took a hard look at the pernicious effects of advertising; and *The Man in the Gray Flannel Suit,* a novel by Sloan Wilson, highlights the struggle to find purpose in a world of corporate conformity. Of the novel, columnist Bob Greene wrote in the *Chicago Tribune* in 1992: "The title of Sloan Wilson's bestselling novel became part of the American vernacular—the book

---

* For the author this is one of those terms that provide more heat than light and that he suspects is a major trigger of migraine headaches among other nonacademics along with deconstructuralism, poststructuralism, and existentialism.

was a ground-breaking fictional look at conformity in the executive suite, and it was a piece of writing that helped the nation's business community start to examine the effects of its perceived stodginess and sameness."

PROSUMER. Futurist **Alvin Toffler** coined *prosumer* in his classic 1980 work *The Third Wave*. Toffler's prosumer combined *producer* and *consumer* and referred to individuals who design the products they purchase. More recently, however, prosumer has been given a second meaning as a portmanteau of *professional* and *consumer*, indicating people who are amateurs in a given field but covet professional-grade equipment such as industrial-grade kitchen equipment and garden machinery.

PROTESTANT WORK ETHIC. First coined by sociologist **Max Weber** (1864–1920) in 1904, who saw work as a duty that benefits both the individual and society as a whole. Also, work that is generally good for physical and mental health and has a positive impact on an individual's well-being.

PSYCHOBABBLE. Psychological jargon regarded as meaningless. A term created by **Richard D. Rosen**, novelist who first used it in a 1975 article in the *Boston Phoenix*: "We are living, practically no one has to be reminded, in a therapeutic age. The sign in every storefront reads: 'Psychobabble spoken here.'" Rosen is also credited with hatching the term *psychobabbler* for one who uses the jargon. The suffix *-babble* is used for the most negative and obfuscatory aspects of jargon. Babble itself started life in the fourteenth century to describe the gurgles and vocables of infants. See also **TECHNOBABBLE**.

PUGILIST. A practitioner of the art of boxing; a boxer, a fighter. This is one of the many words debuted by **Pierce Egan** (1772–1849), the man who can be regarded as the first beat sports reporter and the first to apply slang (some of his own making) to the low sports—boxing, cockfighting, bullbaiting.[6]

PUNDUSTRY. The pundit industry. The term was coined by columnist **Gene Weingarten** in his cover story for the *Washington Post* magazine for March 23, 2008, entitled "Cruel and Unusual Punishment," an allusion to the fact that he forced himself to watch five televisions simultaneously, each containing a different political pundit opining on the same subject. The *pundustry* as Weingarten saw it: "There are too many voices, competing too hard, fighting for attention, ranting, redundant, random. The dissemination of fact and opinion is no longer the sole province of people and institutions with the money to buy network monopolies or ink by the ton, as it was a half-century ago when information was delivered to us, for better or worse, like the latest 1950s-era cigarette: filtered, for an illusion of safety. Now, all is out of control. Everyone with a computer is a potential pundit; anyone with a video camera can be on a screen."

PUSHMI-PULLYU. An imaginary creature resembling a llama or antelope, but with a head at either end of the body, pointing away from the torso, so that the creature always faces in two directions at once. It was created in 1922 by British children's author **Hugh Lofting** (1886–1947) for his book *Doctor Dolittle*, in which he noted that "pushmi-pullyus are now extinct ... They had no tail, but a head at each end, and sharp horns on each head ... Only one half of him slept at a time. The other head was always awake—and watching." The name of the beast is often invoked to describe policies, e.g., "The constitutional division of war powers is not intended to produce a pushmi-pullyu, with two minds to make up."[7]

QUARK. A word that first appears in **James Joyce**'s *Finnegans Wake* in the nonce phrase "Three Quarks for Muster Mark" but that was reapplied as the name for any of a group of elementary particles supposed to be the fundamental units that combine to make up the subatomic particles known as hadrons. Scientist Murray Gell-Mann had been thinking about calling the unit "kwork," but when he found the invented word in the Joyce classic, he knew he had discovered the spelling he wanted to use. Here's what he had to say about it: "In 1963, when I assigned the name 'quark' to the fundamental constituents of the nucleon, I had the sound first, without the spelling, which could have been 'kwork.' Then, in one of my occasional perusals of *Finnegans Wake*, by James Joyce, I came across the word 'quark.'"[1]

QUATRESSENTIAL. Not quite quintessential. One of a number of new words that American writer **Lewis Burke Frumkes** has offered the English language via his article, "A Volley of Words," in *Harper's* magazine. Two other examples of

Frumkes's fine work: *copulescence*, the healthy afterglow that attends successful sexual intercourse; *ossis*, the contents of a black hole.

QUIDDITCH. An imaginary game in which players fly on broomsticks. The game is played in **J. K. Rowling**'s Harry Potter novels. The term was added to the sixth edition of the *Collins English Dictionary* because its editor said it is an example of a word created for fiction but is understood even by those who have not read the books or seen the films

QUIXOTIC. Exceedingly idealistic; unrealistic and impractical. Eponym based on Don Quixote, the name of the hero of the satirical romance by **Miguel de Cervantes** (1547–1616), published in two parts in 1605 and 1615. The term made its debut in the writing of British satirist and political writer **Nicholas Amhurst** (1697–1742) in the lines: "Pulpit and Press fictitious Ills engage, And combat Windmills with *Quixotic* Rage," alluding to the ultimate Quixotic metaphor "tilting at windmills."[2]

RADICAL CHIC. Created by **Tom Wolfe** in his 1970 essay about fund-raising events, hosted by the rich and famous, for the revolutionary Black Panthers. The term became generalized to refer to the support of radical causes by fashionable and/or wealthy patrons as evidence of their trendiness.

RATOMORPHIC. **Arthur Koestler**'s term for a view of human behavior modeled on the behavior of laboratory rats and other experimental animals.

RESISTENTIALISM. Name for a mock-academic theory to describe "seemingly spiteful behavior manifested by inanimate objects." In other words, a war is being fought between humans and inanimate objects, and all the little annoyances objects inflict on people throughout the day are battles between the two. The term was coined by British humorist **Paul Jennings** in a piece titled "Report on Resistentialism," published in the *Spectator* in April 1948 and reprinted in the *New York Times* and elsewhere. The slogan of *resistentialism* is "Les choses sont contre nous"—"Things are against us." In an essay on the subject in the *New York Times* for September 21, 2003, Charles Harrington Elster called resistentialism "a brilliant send-up of Jean-Paul Sartre and the philosophy of existentialism."

RETROMINGENT. Urinating backward. This term was not coined by **Ben Bradlee**, executive editor of the *Washington Post*, but was given new life when he employed it as a term of derogation in a letter to pesky media critic Reed Irvine of Accuracy in Media. In the spring of 1978, Bradlee became fed up with Reed's rantings and wrote him in part: "You have revealed yourself as a miserable, carping, retromingent vigilante and I for one am sick of wasting my time communicating with you." As Bradlee recalled in his 1996 autobiography, *A Good Life:* "God knows where I found '*retromingent*' but it was the perfect word for the occasion, describing that subspecies of ants (and other animals) which urinate backwards. His supporters were outraged." Irvine parlayed the insult into hundreds of thousands of dollars in contributions.[1]

RETRONYM. A new name for an object or concept to differentiate its original form or version from a more recent form or version. The term was coined by journalist **Frank Mankiewicz** and was first brought to public attention in a 1980 column by William Safire. More than twenty-five years later Safire wrote that Mankiewicz, who in 1980 was president of National Public Radio, had coined the word in response to the evolution of book formats: "He was especially intrigued by the usage *hardcover book*, which was originally a plain book until soft cover books came along, which were originally called paperback and now have spawned a version the size of a hardcover but with a soft cover trade-named with the retronym trade paperback." Other examples include landline telephone, acoustic guitar, whole milk, film camera, World War I and regular coffee." See also the entry for **BACRONYM**.

ROBOT. Coinage of Czech writer **Karel Čapek**'s (1890–1938) in his 1921 work *R.U.R. (Rossum's Universal Robots)*. Čapek took the Czech term for "serf labor" and adopted it to the animatrons that we think of today. Isaac Asimov invented the words *robotic* and *robotics* after Čapek, in 1941.

ROMEO. A man who embodies the characteristics of Romeo in the play *Romeo and Juliet*. Although it is commonly assumed

Chewing Tobacco package label showing Romeo and Juliet embracing, by an open window, as they are taking leave of each other.

that this character was begat in the play by William Shakespeare, the story of Romeo and Juliet originated in European folklore and was developed by a series of writers in the fifteenth and sixteenth centuries. According to the *OED:* "The first version of the story in which the male lover is called *Romeo* is the Italian novella *Hystoria nouellamente ritrouata di due nobili amanti* by **Luigi da Porto** (1486–1529) which was published posthumously in 1530.

ROOMSCANITIS. An affliction of some partygoers that makes their eyes flit about looking for someone more interesting or less dull than the one they are talking to. Created by **John H. Corcoran Jr.**, who introduced it in an article in the *Washingtonian* magazine in 1975.

RUNCIBLE. Word of uncertain meaning that **Edward Lear** (1812–1888) used to modify such words as *hat, cat, goose,* and *spoon.* It is first employed in 1870 in the poem "The Owl and the Pussy-Cat" in *Poetry for Young People*: "They dined on mince and slices of quince, which they ate with a runcible spoon." In the January 11, 1913, issue of the *Emporia (Kansas) Gazette,* William Allen White wrote of the word's creator: "Lear … was a dear, delicious, crotchety, runcible man, to use one of his own words."

SAD SACK. General term for a misfit. From the name for a cartoon character created for *Yank* magazine by American cartoonist **George Baker** (1915–1975) in 1942 for a hapless and blundering army private.[1]

SALAD DAYS. The term originates in **Shakespeare**'s *Antony and Cleopatra:*

> My salad days,
> When I was green in judgment.

SANDWICH BOARDS. An advertising sign consisting of two placards fastened together at the top with straps supported on the shoulders of the carrier, or sandwich man. Term created or at least so described in print by **Charles Dickens**, who described these advertisers as "a piece of human flesh between two slices of paste board."

SCAREDY-CAT. A timid person; a coward. Introduced in 1933 by US author **Dorothy Parker** in a short story "The Waltz" with this line: "Oh, yes, do let's dance together. It's so nice to meet a man who isn't scaredy-cat about catching my beri-beri."

SCIENTIST. The word was coined in 1840 by the **Rev. William Whewell** (1794–1866) in his book *The Philosophy of the Inductive Sciences,* which contained a seventy-page section on the Language of Science. In

Dorothy Parker

it he discusses how the new words of science should be constructed. He then coins the universally accepted term *physicist,* remarking that the existing term *physician* cannot be used in that sense. He then moves on to the larger concept. "We need very much a name to describe a cultivator of science in general. I should incline to call him a scientist." The word that *scientist* replaced was *philosopher.* An account of this coinage in *Word Study,* a newsletter published by Merriam-Webster in 1948, noted: "Few deliberately invented words have gained such wide currency, and many people will be surprised to learn that it is just over a century old."[2]

SCROLLOPING. Characterized by or possessing heavy, florid ornament. Also proceeding in involutions, rambling. A creation of **Virginia Woolf.**

SCROOGE. A meanspirited miserly person; a skinflint. After the character Ebenezer Scrooge in Charles Dickens's 1843 story "A Christmas Carol." It was only with the world-wide popularity of Dickens's story—often performed as a play—that the name of the character began to be used allegorically. The first example from the *OED* is 1940.

SEMANTICS. The branch of linguistics and logic concerned with meaning is a concept and a term created by **Michel Bréal** (1832–1915), a professor of comparative grammar in Paris, who coined the word in the title of his 1895 *Essai de sémantique (sciencedes significations)*. He also created the modern marathon for the relaunched Olympic Games in Athens in 1896, the same event that has enjoyed worldwide popularity ever since.[3]

SEMORDNILAP. A word that spells another word in reverse. It is the creation of American writer **Willard R. Espy** (1910–1999), who made it by spelling *palindromes* backward. A palindrome is, of course, a word, phrase, or passage that spells the same thing forward as backward. Some choice *semordnilaps*: *straw*, *reknits*, *doom*, and *repaid*. Some trademarks are semiordnilaps: Serutan is intentional, whereas Tums probably is not. One can make the case that if we have gone far enough to accept semordnilap, we can go one step further to embrace *quasisemordnilap* for words that come close to spelling something else backward. A good example is *air raid*.

SERENDIPITY. The writer and politician **Horace Walpole** (1717–1797) invented the word in 1754 as an allusion to

Serendip, an old name for Sri Lanka. Walpole was a prolific letter writer, and he explained to one of his main correspondents that he had based the word on the title of a fairy tale, *The Three Princes of Serendip*. The three princes were always making discoveries, by accidents and sagacity, of things they were not in quest of. The wonderfully onomatopoeic *serendipity*, which is indeed often chosen as Britons' favorite English word when such surveys are taken (alongside *nincompoop* and *discombobulate*), means the making of happy and unexpected discoveries by accident. Incidentally, the original Persian name for Sri Lanka (and in earlier times Ceylon) was Sarandib, a corruption of the Sanskrit name Sinhala Dvipa which literally meant "the island where lions dwell." Sinhalese, or Sinhala, is still the name of one of Sri Lanka's national languages, the other being Tamil.

Walpole holds the honor of writing the first gothic novel, *The Castle of Otranto*, in 1765. It was suggested by a dream he had had and of which "all I could recover was, that I had thought myself in an ancient castle (a very natural dream for a head like mine, filled with Gothic story), and that on the uppermost banister of a great staircase I saw a gigantic hand in armour."

SHAKEN NOT STIRRED. Proper method for making a perfect martini in the orthodoxy of James Bond, the superspy who was created by **Ian Fleming** and operating under the code name 007. The rule was in direct contrast to W. Somerset Maugham's dictum that "martinis should always be stirred, not shaken, so that the molecules lie sensuously one on top of the other." Bond ordered his *shaken, not stirred*, which he claimed created a colder martini and was the key to avoiding "bruising the gin." In the first installment of the series of Bond novels, *Casino Royale*, 007 doles out specific instructions to the barman on how to prepare his drink, a cocktail that would later become known as the Vesper, after double agent Vesper Lynd. The recipe: three measures of Gordon's gin, one measure of vodka, half a measure of Kina Lillet, with a slice of lemon—shaken. He explains after first ordering the drink: "I never have more than one drink before dinner. But I do like that one to be large and very strong and very cold, and very well-made. I hate small portions of anything, particularly when they taste bad. This drink's my own invention. I'm going to patent it when I think of a good name."[4]*

SHOOT ONESELF IN THE FOOT. In the metaphoric sense of making one's own situation worse. This expression was first used in this sense by anthropologist **William White Howells** (1908-2005) in his 1959 book on human evolution called *Mankind in the Making*: "Certain common useful phrases can be dangerous . . . Like guns, they will do the right thing in the right hands, but they are loaded, and ordinary citizens without Ph.D.'s are not the only ones who have accidents with them. Many a specialist has shot himself in the foot when he thought he was only cleaning a paragraph."[5]

SHOTGUN WEDDING. A wedding made in haste or under duress by reason of the bride's pregnancy. The term and

---

* Later in the same novel Bond, after losing millions of dollars in a game of poker, is asked if he wants his martini shaken or stirred, and snaps, "Do I look like I give a damn?"

the concept were introduced in print by **Sinclair Lewis** in 1927 in his novel *Elmer Gantry*: "There were, in those parts and those days, not infrequent ceremonies known as 'shotgun weddings.'"[6]

SIGNIFICA. Term created by **Irving Wallace** (1916–1990), his daughter, **Amy**, and his son, **David Wallechinsky**, for "unusual or little-known facts which have too much significance to qualify as mere trivia."

SILENT SPRING. A metaphor for environmental disaster from the title of the 1962 book of the same title by American marine biologist and conservationist **Rachel Carson** (1907–1964). She predicted a spring without songbirds if the food chain was destroyed by the unrestrained use of pesticides and herbicides. Carson's book became one of the rallying points for the nascent environmental movement.

SLAM DUNK. Coined in 1972 by Los Angeles Lakers basketball broadcaster **Chick Hearn** (1916–2002) for a basketball shot that is performed when a player jumps in the air and manually powers the ball downward through the basket with one or both hands over the rim.

SLOUGH OF DESPOND. A bout of deep depression—either personal or societal. A *slough* (rhymes with cow) is a muddy, dark bog into which humans wander and get stuck and *despond* is a state of despondency. English Christian writer and preacher **John Bunyan** (1628–1688) introduced the phrase in *Pilgrim's Progress,* where it was a hazard experienced by

Everyman, the main character, on his pilgrimage to the Celestial City.

SMILET. A half smile. A coinage of **William Shakespeare** that debuts with these lines in the fourth act, scene 3, of *King Lear*:

> Those happy *smilets*,
> That play'd on her ripe lip, seem'd not to know
> What guests were in her eyes.

This is one of Shakespeare's words that never became popular. Charles and Mary Cowden Clarke argued for its wider adoption in *The Shakespeare Key:* "We owe to Shakespeare's need of an expressive and poetical word in this passage, descriptive of a tender daughter struggling with her tears and striving to retain patient submission amid her sorrow, the beautiful diminutive 'smilets,' which so well designates attempted smiles, half smiles."[7]

SMIRT. The title of a 1934 novel by **James Branch Cabell** (1879–1958) that the author saw as a fresh expletive. He explained, "There was never any name so impertinent and insulting in sound. It ought to be an invaluable addition to the list of Anglo-Saxon epithets, and if it isn't obscene, it certainly sounds like it." According to the March 1934 issue of *Vanity Fair*, it is supposed to have taken the author two years to think of the title.

SMUTHOUND. Term created by **H. L. Mencken** for censor, "a word superbly suited for expectoration" according to Robert McHugh, editor of *The Bathtub Hoax, and Other Blasts and Bravos from the* Chicago Tribune.[8]

SNOB. There are three separate meanings of this term: (1) a cobbler or cobbler's assistant; (2) a person who imitates, fawningly admires, or vulgarly seeks association with those regarded as social superiors; and (3) a person who tends to rebuff, avoid, or ignore those regarded as inferior. The first meaning is of obscure origin but the other two are prime authorisms. The meaning of snob was coined by **William Makepeace Thackeray** and used in his satirical *Book of Snobs*. "I mean by positive [Snobs], such persons as are Snobs everywhere . . . being by nature endowed with Snobbishness." As for the snob who looks down on others, that usage was introduced in 1911 in George Bernard Shaw's *Getting Married*: "All her childish affectations of conscientious scruple and religious impulse have been applauded and deferred to until she has become an ethical snob of the first water."

SOLD DOWN THE RIVER. To suffer a great betrayal; to be destroyed by the bad faith of another, especially one who you trusted. The exact term and the action from which the metaphor derives is from **Harriet Beecher Stowe's** (1811–1896) *Uncle Tom's Cabin*, which describes in heartrending detail the tragic breakup of black Kentucky families who were actually sold to plantations farther down the Mississippi River where conditions were harsher. The term existed before

Stowe used it but she infused it with a sense of tragedy and betrayal.[9]

SPACE. **John Milton**, who visited Galileo in 1638, was also the first writer to ever use the word *space*, in the sense of *outer space*, to consider the infinite scope of the universe. As he wrote in book 8 of *Paradise Lost*:

> ... this earth a spot, a grain,
> An atom, with the firmament compared
> And all her numbered stars that seem to roll
> Space incomprehensible (for such
> Their distance argues and their swift return
> Diurnal).[10]

SPARROW FART. A person or thing of no consequence. **James Joyce** wrote about Penelope in *Ulysses,* episode 18: "Miss This Miss That Miss the other lot of sparrowfarts skitting around talking about politics they know as much about as my backside." It is a word that is rarely used but can be employed to great effect as in this line from Kurt Vonnegut's *God Bless You, Mr. Rosewater:* "The hell with the talented sparrowfarts who write delicately of one small piece of one mere lifetime, when the issues are galaxies, eons, and trillions of souls yet to be born." It should be added that the term DUCK FART is a baseball term for a bloop single. The term was coined by Chicago White Sox announcer **Ken Harrelson** because the sound made by the ball coming off the bat is presumably similar to how he imagined the sound made by a duck farting (rather than a solid "crack").

-SPEAK. Suffix appended to words to denote a specialized way of speaking; a particular jargon or slang. The construction is drawn from **George Orwell**'s *1984* in which there are two languages: Oldspeak, which is English as we know it and Newspeak, which is sterile language that serves the needs of a totalitarian state. The term is introduced in Orwell's 1949 novel: "Syme was a philologist, a specialist in Newspeak. Indeed, he was one of the enormous team of experts now engaged in compiling the Eleventh Edition of the Newspeak Dictionary."

Hundreds of examples have been created in the wake of Orwell's neologism, including *Newtspeak* and *Bushspeak,* the later attributed to presidents George H. W. Bush and George W. Bush, the former alluding to former U.S. Speaker of the House of Representatives Newt Gingrich.

SPIFFLICATED. Intoxicated, drunk. One of close to three thousand known and documented synonyms for drunk, this one is the creation of **O. Henry** and first appears in his 1906 short story collection *The Four Million*: "He uses Nature's Own Remedy. He gets spifflicated."

SPINACHY. Characteristic or suggestive of a dark leafy vegetable. A nonce word created by **Ogden Nash** for a poem in his 1950 collection *Family Reunion*:

So spinach was too spinachy
For Leonardo da Vinaci.

STAGGERMENT. Great amazement or astonishment that is enough to change one's gait. It is one of **J. R. R. Tolkien**'s nonce words.[11]

STAR-CROSS'D. Coined by **William Shakespeare** to describe the young lovers in the prologue to *Romeo and Juliet*:

> Two households, both alike in dignity,
> In fair Verona, where we lay our scene,
> From ancient grudge break to new mutiny,
> Where civil blood makes civil hands unclean.
> From forth the fatal loins of these two foes
> A pair of star-cross'd lovers take their life.

The term has come to describe two people whose tragic destinies are intertwined. *Cross'd* has special impact in that it carries and connotes the triple meanings of (1) brought into each other's path, (2) thwarted, and (3) burdened (as in *a cross to bear*).

STEREOTYPE. A preconceived and oversimplified notion of the characteristics that typify a person, situation. Stereotype originally was a printing term for a relief printing plate that was cast in a mold made from composed type or an original plate. The word was redefined by American newspaper columnist **Walter Lippmann** (1889–1974) in 1922 in his book *Public Opinion*. He called a stereotype an "intellectual crutch, a substitute for precise analysis and an excuse for not viewing individuals and historical eras singularly, as they actually are." Lippmann used the term to describe the fixed and harmful images that various European nationalities stubbornly held of each other and that, he believed, helped incline them to go to war. "A stereotype may be so consistently and authoritatively transmitted in each generation from parent to child that it seems almost like a biological fact."[12]

STRINE. Coined by **Alistair Morrison** to represent an alleged Australian pronunciation of *Australian*. Writing under the pseudonym Afferbeck Lauder (echoic of *alphabetical order*) and as professor of strine studies at the University of Sinny (Sydney), Morrison published a series of humorous articles in the *Sydney Morning Herald*, some of which were later collected and published under the title *Let Stalk Strine* in 1965.

STUD MUFFIN. Term for a sexually attractive male often used with a trace of derogation. It was created by American humorist **Dave Barry** and first included in his syndicated newspaper column January 9, 1986: "In Washington, House and Senate budget conferees agree to call each other by nicknames such as 'Stud Muffin.'"

STUFFED SHIRT. American novelist **Willa Cather**'s (1873–1947) term for one who is pompous and conservative, but usually ineffectual. Cather first used it in 1913 in *O Pioneers!*: "He characterized Frank Shabata by a Bohemian expression which is the equivalent of stuffed shirt."[13]

SUBTERRANEAN. The term *subterranean* was used by some to describe the 1950s bohemians. Jack Kerouac's 1958 novel, *The Subterraneans*, is a portrait of the bohemian subculture of New York and San Francisco. Kerouac wrote that the term was a "name invented by Adam Moorad [the name Kerouac used for Allen Ginsberg in *The Subterraneans*] who is a poet and friend of mine," and that John Clellon Holmes referred to them as "urban Thoreaus." Appearing at the Kaye Playhouse at Hunter College in 1958, Kerouac said, "And now there are two types of beat hipsters—the Cool: bearded, sitting without moving in cafes, with their unfriendly girls dressed in black, who say nothing, and the Hot: Crazy, talkative, mad shining eyes, running from bar to bar only to be ignored by the cool subterranean."

SUINE. A **James Joyce** nonce word for *piglike*, created for *Ulysses*: "The suine scions of the house of Lambert."[14]

SUPPLY-SIDE ECONOMICS. A theory and term created by journalist **Jude Wanniski** (1936–2005) to describe a school of economic theory that stresses the costs of production as a means of stimulating the economy and advocates policies that raise capital and labor output by increasing the incentive to produce. It promotes big tax cuts as the best cure for an ailing economy.

SUPERLAWYER. The term appeared as the title of a bestselling 1972 book by **Joseph C. Goulden**, who recalls, "As far as I know, I am the first person to use the term in print. During an interview in which a lawyer specializing in transportation issues sought to dispel the notion that Washington attorneys are somehow different—his name has long-since slipped through a crevice in my memory, never to be seen again—told me: 'All I do, really, is practice law. It's nothing different from what my Yale classmates do in Boston or Philadelphia or Chicago. I research and write briefs and argue my cases, and try to keep my clients happy, and I cut the grass every second Saturday. I'm not a Superlawyer, I'm not a man who backslaps John Mitchell [then the attorney general] or George Romney [then the governor of Michigan]—hell, the most influential man I've met this year is an assistant secretary of transportation who goes to our church.'"

SURREALISM. Italian-born French poet **Guillaume Apollinaire** (1880–1918) coined the word to describe the fusion of radically new arts, in a review of the ballet *Parade*, which had a script by Jean Cocteau, scenography by Pablo Picasso, music by Erik Satie, and choreography by Léonide Massine. Apollinaire created his own surrealist play, *Les Mamelles de Tirésias*, staged in June 1917.[15]

SURVIVAL OF THE FITTEST. Although commonly associated with Charles Darwin, the phrase was coined by **Herbert Spencer** (1820–1903), an English philosopher. It is the process by which organisms that are less well adapted to their environment tend to perish and better-adapted organisms tend to survive. Unlike Charles Darwin, for whom evolution was without direction or morality, Spencer believed evolution to be both progressive and good.

SVENGALI. A person who exerts power over another through the force of personality or will. It is the name of a character in **George du Maurier**'s (1834–1896) 1894 novel *Trilby*, in which the title character, a beautiful woman, falls under the spell of Svengali who employs hypnotism to turn her into a great singer.

SYNONYMOMANIA. A word created by **Theodore M. Bernstein** to describe the "compulsion to call a spade successively a garden implement and an earth-turning tool." Both this term and the complementary monologophobia appear in Bernstein's *The Careful Writer*.

T

T-SHIRT. The name of this torso-covering undergarment certainly comes from its T shape and was not introduced in the United States until World War I when they were modeled on similar garments worn by European soldiers. The first citing of the term given by the *OED* is by **F. Scott Fitzgerald** in 1920 in *This Side of Paradise:* "Amory, provided with 'six suits summer underwear ... one sweater or T shirt,' set out for New England, the land of schools."[1]

TABOO (TABU). Forbidden. Imported into English by British explorer **Captain James Cook** (1728–1779) in 1777 in his *Journal of a Voyage Round the World in H.M.S. Endeavour 1768–1771.* He wrote of a dinner at Tongataboo, a Polynesian island: "When dinner came on table not one of my guests would sit down or eat a bit of any thing that was there. Every one was *Tabu*, a word of a very comprehensive meaning but in general signifies forbidden."[2]

TAR BABY. A problem that clings to you no matter what you do to get rid of it. The original *tar baby* is a doll covered with tar that appears in American journalist, fiction writer, and folklorist **Joel Chandler Harris**'s (1848–1908) *Uncle Remus,* his first book of stories published in 1881. In the story of the tar baby, Brer Rabbit attempts to speak to the tar baby, which does not answer. He becomes angry and hits the tar baby, which sticks to him. The more he tries to punch the doll, the tighter it sticks to him. *Tar Baby* was also used by Toni Morrison as the title for her 1981 book that used it as a metaphor for strength. "At one time," she said in a 1995 interview when asked to explain the title, "a tar pit was a holy place, at least an important place, because tar was used to build things. It held together things like Moses' little boat and the pyramids. For me, the tar baby came to mean the black woman who can hold things together."[3]

TARZAN. Name for a person with real or imagined strength and agility. It comes from the name of the main character in a series of novels by American novelist **Edgar Rice Burroughs** (1875–1950), and in subsequent films and television series. Tarzan was orphaned in West Africa in his infancy and reared in the jungle by a mother ape. The character is introduced to the world in 1914 in the book *Tarzan of the Apes.* Burroughs was the first writer to incorporate himself, which he did in 1923. Edgar Rice Burroughs, Inc. of Tarzana, California, still manages his properties.

TECHNOBABBLE. Empty and/or obfuscatory technical talk from the title of **John Barry**'s 1976 book of the same title. The term was later blended with *trek* to form *treknobabble* to describe the particular technical gibberish employed in the various *Star Trek* series such as the dilithium crystals, which are used to power starships in the *Star Trek* universe.

TERMINOLOGICAL INEXACTITUDE. Winston Churchill's 1906 euphemism for lying.

THE AMERICAN DREAM. Phrase coined by American writer and historian **James Truslow Adams** (1878–1949) in 1931 in his book *The Epic of America* as "that dream of a land in which life should be better and richer and fuller for everyone, with opportunity for each according to ability or achievement. It is a difficult dream for the European upper classes to interpret adequately, and too many of us ourselves have grown weary and mistrustful of it. It is not a dream of motor cars and high wages merely, but a dream of social order in which each man and each woman shall be able to attain to the fullest stature of which they are innately capable, and be recognized by others for what they are, regardless of the fortuitous circumstances of birth or position." The term and the concept have been fodder for playwrights who have explored what they see as its false promise: Edward Albee in his 1961 *The American Dream* and Arthur Miller's 1949 *Death of a Salesman* among others.

THE BACK OF BEYOND. A lonely forsaken place, real or imagined. It was first put into print by **Sir Walter Scott** in his novel *The Antiquary*, 1816: "You ... whirled them to the back of beyond to look at the auld Roman camp."

THE BEST AND THE BRIGHTEST. Term for the cream of the crop but sometimes employed ironically to describe leaders who are, for whatever reason or reasons, led to make gross errors in judgment. It is the title of **David Halberstam**'s (1934-2007) 1972 book about the policy makers who brought the United States into the Vietnam War.

THE EARTH MOVED. A metaphoric phrase for sexual fulfillment coined by **Ernest Hemingway** in his 1926 novel *For Whom the Bell Tolls*. In the story, Hemingway's American hero, Robert Jordan, is fighting on the side of a guerrilla band of Spanish Loyalists against the Fascists; he makes love to Maria, a young woman who had been mistreated by the guerrillas. Then Jordan asks, "But did thee feel the earth move?" She replied, yes. Later when pressed by one of the guerrilla leaders to tell what happened, she states only that "the earth moved."

THE KING'S ENGLISH. Name for English as it is spoken and written by educated people in southern England. It appears first in **William Shakespeare**'s *The Merry Wives of Windsor:* "Here will be an old abusing of God's patience and the king's English." *Merry Wives* is Shakespeare's only play set in England.

THE LIGHT FANTASTIC. John Milton coined "the light fantastic" to describe dancing in 1632.

THE PERFECT STORM. A true lexical curiosity in that the *Oxford English Dictionary* recognized this as a positive metaphoric term ("a perfect storm of applause") before it became a meteorological one. It is often misattributed to William Makepeace Thackery, who used it as an affirmation in his novel *Vanity Fair.**

Sebastian Junger's *The Perfect Storm: A True Story of Men Against the Sea*, published in 1997, recounts the story of the October 1991 *perfect storm* that caused the loss of the Gloucester fishing boat *Andrea Gail* off the Nova Scotia coast. The general use of the term in the negative metaphoric sense stems from Junger's book and has come to have a meaning akin to "worst case scenario." It was invoked so many times to describe the financial crisis that began in 2007 that it was awarded that year's top prize by Lake Superior State University in its list of words that deserve to be banned for overuse.

THE RIGHT STUFF. The character, courage, and savvy of test pilots and astronauts from the name of the 1979 bestselling book by **Tom Wolfe** and a 1983 movie based on the book. It can be argued that this may be the primary honorific of the space age, invoked sparingly in its original sense such as when it was applied to the crews of the *Columbia* and *Challenger*

---

* The passage in full: "I have heard a brother of the story-telling trade at Naples preaching to a pack of good-for-nothing honest, lazy fellows by the sea-shore, work himself up into such a rage and passion with some of the villains whose wicked deeds he was describing and inventing, that the audience could not resist it; and they and the poet together would burst out into a roar of oaths and execrations against the fictitious monster of the tale, so that the hat went round, and the bajocchi tumbled into it, in the midst of a perfect storm of sympathy."

disasters. But when used more commonly it becomes little more than a public relations buzzword, as in, for example, a September 16, 2002, press release from NASA titled "The Right Stuff for Super Spaceships: Tomorrow's Spacecraft Will Be Built Using Advanced Materials with Mind-Boggling Properties."

Wolfe did not create the term. The earliest use of the term in the modern sense appears in the writing of **James Fenimore Cooper** in an article in the May 1845 issue of *Graham's American Monthly Magazine of Literature, Art and Fashion,* in a biographical essay on Edward Preble. In attesting to Preble's "courage, determination and high temper," Cooper tells an anecdote in which Preble throws stones at a boating party that included his father, General Jedediah Preble, who had promised to board him then later refused. "It seems the old general decided that the boy had the 'Right Stuff' in him, and overlooked the gross impropriety of the assault, on account of its justice and spirit."[*]

Tom Wolfe resurrected the phrase to describe the mystique of flying associated with test pilots and the first men in space

---

[*] The term was used in this sense for humans and also for horses to describe racehorses with the ability to run. A horse named Miracle Sub is described in the Bettors Edge tip sheet in the *Chicago Defender* for July 9, 1975, as having the "Right Stuff."

as the subhead for a series of four 1973 articles in *Rolling Stone* magazine called "Post-Orbital Remorse—The Brotherhood of The Right Stuff."[4]

THE SHOT HEARD ROUND THE WORLD. The phrase first appeared in **Ralph Waldo Emerson**'s song "Concord Hymn," which was sung at the dedication of the monument in Concord, Massachusetts, commemorating the April 19, 1775, battles of Lexington and Concord.

THE SYSTEM. Introduced by muckraker **Thomas William Lawson** (1857–1925) in his series "Frenzied Finance" in *Everybody's Magazine*. It pertains to stock manipulation and trusts in general.

THO. The word *though* as it was spelled at the *Chicago Tribune* between 1934 and 1975. **Colonel Robert McCormick**, the publisher of the paper, instituted spelling reforms in fits and starts, with varying degrees of success. In July 2010, Graham Meyer wrote in *Chicago* magazine, "Almost everyone today accepts *catalog* and *tranquility* but *frate* and *iland* not so much."

THON. A word coined in 1858 by American attorney and composer of church music **C. C. Converse** (1832–1918) as a neutral pronoun of the third person, common gender, a contracted and solidified form of *that one* as a substitute in cases in which the use of a restrictive pronoun (his/her) involves either inaccuracy or obscurity, where its nonemployment necessitates awkward repetition (his or her). For examples "If Harry or his wife comes, I will be on hand to meet thon [for the one who comes.]." "Each pupil must learn thon's lesson [for his or her own]."

TIGHTWAD. A miserly person; one who keeps his wad of paper money tightly rolled. This word first appears in 1900 in **George Ade**'s *More Fables*, a book in which familiar stories were told in slang.

TINTINNABULATION. **Edgar Allan Poe** popularized the term in 1831 for the sound of bells in the first stanza of his poem "The Bells":

> Hear the sledges with the bells—
> Silver bells!
> What a world of merriment their melody foretells!
> How they tinkle, tinkle, tinkle,
> In the icy air of night!
> While the stars that oversprinkle
> All the heavens, seem to twinkle
> With a crystalline delight;
> Keeping time, time, time,
> In a sort of Runic rhyme,
> To the tintinnabulation that so musically wells
> From the bells, bells, bells, bells,
> Bells, bells, bells—
> From the jingling and the tinkling of the bells.

TO THE MANNER BORN. A **Shakespearean** construction from *Hamlet* meaning to be naturally accustomed to a certain way of doing things. The expression comes from *Hamlet*, act 1, scene 4, when Hamlet observes of the drunken atmosphere at Elsinore:

> But to my mind, though I am native here
> And to the manner born, it is a custom
> More honour'd in the breach than the observance.

The phrase allows for punning, as in the BBC comedy series *To the Manor Born,* which ran from 1979 to 1981 and was also one of the classic "Britcom" hits on American PBS.

TRISKAIDEKAPHOBIA. Morbid or irrational fear of the number 13. Coined by American psychiatrist and neurologist **Isador Henry Coriat** (1875–1943) from the Greek *tris* (3), *kai* (and), *deca* (10), and *phobia* (morbid fear).

TROGGLEHUMPER. A nightmare in the world created by **Roald Dahl**, who also called them *bogthumpers* and *grobswitchers* as opposed to his names for pleasant dreams, which were known by melodious names of *winksquiffers* and *phizzwizards.*

TRUTHINESS. As defined by its coiner American political comedian **Stephen Colbert**, "truth that comes from the gut, not books" and introduced on Comedy Central's *The Colbert Report* in October 2005. The word was so popular that it eventually became *Merriam-Webster's* number one Word of the Year for 2006 and was awarded the sixteenth annual Word of the Year by the American Dialect Society, and defined by them as "the quality of preferring concepts or facts one wishes to be true, rather than concepts or facts known to be true." *Truthiness* begat *truthy*: in 2010, the *New York Times* discussed the status of political discourse saying that extensive effort goes into "disentangling reliable political Twitter posts from those that are merely truthy."

TSUNAMI. A brief series of long, high undulations on the surface of the sea caused by an earthquake or similar underwater disturbance often and until recently known by the misnomer tidal wave. This is a term that was first imported into English from the Japanese by author and translator **Lafcadio Hearn** (1850–1904), known also by the Japanese name Koizumi Yakumo. Hearn was an international writer, known best for his books about Japan. This is his introductory line from 1897, which appears in his book *Gleanings in Buddha-Fields:* "'*Tsunami!*' shrieked the people; and then all shrieks and all sounds and all power to hear sounds were annihilated by a nameless shock ... as the colossal swell smote the shore with a weight that sent a shudder through the hills."[5]

TULGEY. Word introduced by **Lewis Carroll** in 1871 in *Through the Looking-Glass* for thick, dense, and dark.

> The Jabberwock, with eyes of flame
> Came whiffling through the tulgey wood.

TWITTER. As a verb this word has several meanings, one of which is to tease. The *OED* attributes the term to **Henry Fielding** in *Tom Jones:* "It doth not become such a one as you to *twitter* me." The modern social network known as Twitter was named by its founder **Jack Dorsey**, who explained the decision to the *Los Angeles Times:* "We came across the word 'twitter,' and it was just perfect. The definition was 'a short burst of inconsequential information,' and 'chirps from birds.' And that's exactly what the product was."[6]

U

UFFISH. A state of being **Lewis Carroll** envisioned as "when the voice is gruffish, the manner roughish, and the temper huffish."

UGLY AMERICAN. Term used to describe an obnoxious Yankee abroad. It comes from the title of a novel by **William J. Lederer** and **Eugene Burdick** in which the term is used to describe an American who was compassionate and idealistic but physically unattractive. The misnomer has prevailed. In a 1988 interview, Costa Rican president Óscar Arias said, "If I had to advise Washington on its policy in Latin America, I'd say, 'Please be nice—please stop being the ugly American.'"[1]

UGLY DUCKLING. Term for a young person who shows no promise of the transformation that will come with maturity. It is an allusion to the story by **Hans Christian Andersen** first translated into English in 1846 called the "The Ugly Duckling." The story tells of a homely little bird born in a barnyard who suffers abuse from the others around him until, much to his delight (and to the surprise of others), he matures into a beautiful swan.

UNBIRTHDAY. A day that is not one's birthday but is nevertheless worthy of celebration. First observed by **Lewis Carroll** in *Through the Looking-Glass:* "'What *is* an un-birthday present?' 'A present given when it isn't your birthday, of course.'"[2]

UNCONSCIOUS. The meaning of this term—being unaware of something existing within oneself—was coined by the eighteenth-century German romantic philosopher **Friedrich Schelling** (1775-1854) and introduced into English in 1816 by the poet and essayist **Samuel Taylor Coleridge** (1772-1834): "Still picturing that look askance, With forc'd unconscious sympathy Full before her father's view." Temporarily devoid of consciousness. The secondary meaning of the term—to be temporarily devoid of consciousness—made its first appearance in 1860 in the writing of **Oliver Wendell Holmes**: "A man is stunned by a blow with a stick on the head. He becomes unconscious."[3]

UNDER TOAD. A form of intense anxiety, the chief feature of which is an overwhelming fear of the unknown in general and of one's personal mortality in particular. This is American novelist **John Irving**'s term for fear of tragedy, coined in his 1976 *The World According to Garp*. In the book, the youngest child, Walt, is constantly being warned to "watch out for the undertow" while playing in the surf, but he mishears the word as *Under Toad*: "Garp . . . realized that all these years Walt had been dreading a giant toad, lurking offshore, waiting to suck him under and drag him out to sea. The terrible Under Toad."

UNDERWORLD. As used to describe the world of organized crime, this term was adopted to print by muckraker **Josiah Flynt** (1869–1910). According to William McKeen, professor and chairman of the Department of Journalism at Boston University, Flynt's articles in the *Century* and *McClure's* were so peppered with colorful expressions and his extensive use of argot, that Flynt has been cited as a force in loosening up the writing of journalists. An alcoholic and drug addict, Flynt is credited with having introduced such terms as "mob" (for organized crime), "squeal" (to inform on another), "speakeasy" (an illegal bar), "fix" (as in a bribe), "handout" (something given free), "pull" (for influence), "pinch" (for arrest), and "joint" (for an illegal establishment).[4]

UNPERSON. An individual who for political or social reasons is deemed not to have existed and whose name is removed from all public records. By extension, one whose existence or achievement is officially denied or disregarded; a person of no political or social importance. Introduced by **George Orwell** in 1949 in *1984*: "Syme was not only dead, he was abolished, an unperson." In American politics, losing candidates often are branded with this label within days of their loss. "Mitt Romney," wrote Michael Hirsh in the *National Journal* of February 14, 2013, "the late lamented presidential candidate (in case you forgot who he was), has quickly become an unperson in a Republican Party that never much wanted him as its champion in the first place."

UNPUTDOWNABLE. The word that supplanted *unlaydownable* after **Raymond Chandler** (1888–1959) said of a book in 1947, "I found it absolutely . . . unputdownable."[6]

UNLAYDOWNABLE. Coinage in the mid-1930s of **Franklin P. Adams,** who maintained that he had found a book of that nature. The term later yielded in popularity to *unputdownable.*[5]

URBANALITY. James Thurber's term for self-conscious and plodding urbanity. He used it to describe, among other things, the early issues of the *New Yorker*.

UTOPIA. The English statesman and author **Sir Thomas More** invented the word *utopia* in his book of the same name, published in 1516. He coined the word from three Greek elements *topos* (place), *eu* (good), and *ou* (no). The idea behind the Greek double meaning was that a utopia was an ideal, perfect place—but that such a place could never exist. According to the *OED*, the antonym *dystopia* is an imaginary place or condition in which everything is as bad as possible. It appears in 1952 in a book called *The Quest for Utopia* by Glenn Robert Negley and John Max Patrick, introduced in this sentence: "The *Mundus Alter et Idem* [of Joseph Hall] is . . . the opposite of *utopia*, the ideal society: it is a *dystopia*, if it is permissible to coin a word." The neologism was applied to such works as George Orwell's *1984* and Aldous Huxley's *Brave New World*.

UTOPIATE. Blend of *utopia* and *opiate* to describe a drug— e.g., LSD—which produces fantasies of a utopian existence; a total escape from reality. Coined by **Richard Hosmer Blum** of Stanford University in 1964 for the title and subject of his book *Utopiates: The Use and Users of LSD 25*: "The movement promises much—a return to paradise, a Utopia of the inner life—and so LSD-25 becomes, if one may be allowed a neologism, a 'Utopiate.'"

V

VAGULATE. To wander in a vague manner; to waver. This **Virginia Woolf** creation is so rare that all three citations in the *OED* for it are from Woolf's writing.[1]

VAGULOUS. Wayward, vague, wavering. This word was also coined by **Virginia Woolf.**

VERBICIDE. British novelist and critic **C. S. Lewis**'s term for the killing of a word or the willful distortion or depreciation of its original meaning. Verbicide is discussed at length in Lewis's *Studies in Words*, making such assertions about the act as this: "But the greatest cause of verbicide is the fact that most people are obviously far more anxious to express their approval and disapproval of things than to describe them. Hence the tendency of words to become less descriptive and more evaluative; then become evaluative, while still retaining some hint of the sort of goodness or badness implied; and to end up by being purely evaluative—useless synonyms for *good* or for *bad*."

VERBIVORE. This neologism first appears in the title of American author and teacher **Richard Lederer**'s 1994 book *Adventures of a Verbivore*. He defined the term: "Carnivores eat flesh and meat; piscivores eat fish; herbivores consume plants and vegetables; verbivores devour words. I am such a creature. My whole life I have feasted on words—ogled their appetizing shapes, colors, and textures; swished them around in my mouth; lingered over their many tastes; felt their juices run down my chin. During my adventures as a fly-by-the-roof-of-the-mouth, user-friendly wizard of idiom, I have met thousands of other wordaholics, logolepts, and verbivores, folks who also eat their words."[2]

VIDEOT. American sportswriter **Red Smith**'s (1905–1982) word for those who watch anything that flickers across the television screen.

VISIBILIA. That which can be seen. A 1936 coinage of **C. S. Lewis**: "On the one hand you can start with an immaterial fact, such as the passions which you actually experience, and can then invent visibilia to express them."[3]

VOMITY. Suggesting vomit. The word made its debut in **J. D. Salinger**'s 1951 *The Catcher in the Rye*, in which the main character Holden Caulfield observes: "The cab I had was a real old one that smelled like someone'd just tossed his cookies in it. I always get those vomity kind of cabs if I go anywhere late at night."

W

WACK. A crazy person. The term made its literary debut in **Ellery Queen**'s *The Four of Hearts:* "All you wacks act this way at first. Them that can take it snaps out of it." Queen is both the fictional hero of the Ellery Queen mysteries as well as the author—the pseudonym for two cousins from Brooklyn, New York, named Daniel Nathan (1905–1982) and Manford (Emanuel) Lepofsky (1905–1971). They also published books under the names **Frederic Dannay** and **Manfred Bennington Lee** respectively.

WALTER MITTY. Eponym for any ordinary, timid person who indulges in daydreams involving great adventures and heroic feats. After the title character in *The Secret Life of Walter Mitty*, the 1939 short story by **James Thurber** was made into a movie of the same name. Thurber's story appeared in the March 18, 1939, issue of the *New Yorker* magazine. In the story, Walter Mitty is a meek husband, rather uxorious, who fantasizes great exploits to escape the humdrum of daily life. One minute he is dreaming of being a heroic pilot ("Throw on the power lights! Rev her up to 8500!"); the next minute he becomes a daring naval commander. In his next thought he transforms into a master surgeon, and even a cold-blooded killer.

WAR PAINT. Pigments applied to the face or body in preparation for battle, as in certain tribal societies; and by extension, the cosmetics such as lipstick, rouge, or mascara applied before social situations. Introduced by **James Fenimore Cooper** in *The Last of the Mohicans*: "The young Huron was in his warpaint." Cooper may well have invented the term.[1]

WARS OF THE ROSES. What we now call the civil wars fought mainly in England and Wales between 1455 and 1485 and were sometimes referred to by contemporaries as the "Cousins' Wars." The *War of the Roses* was coined by **Sir Walter Scott** in his novel *Anne of Geierstein*, published in 1829.

WASP. Acronym for White Anglo-Saxon Protestant made popular by University of Pennsylvania sociologist **E. Digby Baltzell** (1915–1996) and used to define an entire ethnicity of which he was a member. According to his *New York Times* obituary: "Repeatedly, Dr. Baltzell has been said to have invented the acronym. But Mrs. Baltzell said in an interview yesterday that he had not originated it. She said that it might never be known who first used it, but that Dr. Baltzell 'explicated and defined it in his writings.'" Baltzell certainly made it better known, particularly in his book *The Protestant Establishment: Aristocracy and Caste in America*.[2]

WEAPONS OF MASS DESTRUCTION. The *Times of London* was the first to use this term in 1937 referring to aerial bombing campaigns of the Spanish Civil War of that year, and in particular, the German attack on the Spanish city of Guernica.

WENDY. J. M. Barrie (1860–1937) popularized this name  for the heroine of his play *Peter Pan*. Earlier the name had been extremely rare and used as a boy's name.

WHAT IS PAST IS PROLOGUE. Coined by **Shakespeare**. As used in *The Tempest* this expression means that history influences and sets the context for the present. It is emblazoned on the National Archives building in Washington and used by some to characterize the future of the Department of State and the conduct of American foreign relations.[3]

WHITE-COLLAR. A worker engaged in nonmanual work who usually works in an office. Introduced by **Upton Sinclair** (1878–1968) in 1919 in *The Brass Check*: "It is a fact with which every union workingman is familiar that his most bitter despisers are the petty underlings of the business world, the poor office-clerks ... who, because they are allowed to wear a white collar ... regard themselves as members of the capitalist class." The term *blue-collar* did not come into play for another decade. The first use in the *OED* is 1929 when the two collars are linked in a bulletin reporting on labor conditions: "No economic subject probably is discussed more frequently than the 'wage question' ... This holds for all groups, white collar and blue collar."[4]

WHITE MAN'S BURDEN. Term coined by **Rudyard Kipling** (1865-1936), the English writer and poet who viewed European imperialism in general and Anglo-American imperialism in particular as the salvation of the nonwhite world. One of Kipling's most famous poems, "The White Man's Burden," was published in 1899. It celebrated the racial superiority of white people and praised the men and women who carried "white" virtues to the "backward" peoples of the world. As Donald H. Dyal reports in his *Historical Dictionary of the Spanish American War,* "Kipling sent the first copy to Theodore Roosevelt, whom he believed was the one American most likely to appreciate it. Roosevelt did."[5]

WHODUNIT. A traditional murder mystery. Book critic **Donald Gordon** created the term in the July 1930 *American News of Books* when he said of a new mystery novel: "*Half-Mast Murder*, by Milward Kennedy—A satisfactory *whodunit.*" The term became so popular that by 1939, according to the Merriam-Webster website, "at least one language pundit had declared it 'already heavily overworked' and predicted it would 'soon be dumped into the taboo bin.' " History has proven that prophecy false, and *whodunit* is still going strong. In attributing this neologism to Gordon, the April 1946 issue of *Word Study* noted: "Apparently, a verbal invention, like the man on the flying trapeze, floats through the air with the greatest of ease."

WIMP. The Wymps were characters in a series of children's books by **Evelyn Sharpe** (1869–1955), who was a key figure in the British women's suffrage movement. She was also a tax resister who was twice imprisoned for her actions including breaking the windows of government offices. In her 1898 book *All the Way to Fairyland*, the Wymps first appear as eponymous characters who loved to play practical jokes but cried when anyone returned the favor. The earliest appearance in the modern sense and spelling appears in George Ade's 1920 collection *Hand-made Fables*. In his 1925 *Arrowsmith*, Sinclair Lewis wrote of "wimpish young men."[6]

WINE-DARK SEA. A noun modified by a compound adjective term from **Homer**, who doted on such constructions as this and others like *far-darting Apollo*. In the September 1936 issue of *Word Study*, it is reported that one of the cofounders of *Time* magazine, Britton Haddon (1838-1929), owned a copy of *The Iliad* in which all of the compound epithets were underlined. *Time* pioneered such double locutions as *legacy-stalking* and telescoped neologisms as *cinemaddict, sophomoron*, and *franchisler*.

WINE, WOMEN, AND SONG. **Lord Byron** used a similar phrase in *Don Juan*: "Let us have wine and woman, mirth and laughter, Sermons and soda water the day after."[7]

WORD WORD. A word that is repeated to distinguish it from a *seemingly* identical word or name, created by **Paul Dickson**. There are situations when it is necessary to repeat a word in order to make sure a reader knows what you are talking about. For instance, you might be asked, "Are you talking about an American Indian or an *Indian Indian?*" Or in distinguishing between the grass that grows on lawns and marijuana: "Oh, you're talking about *grass grass*. I thought you were talking about grass." Word words are necessary in an increasingly digital universe—e. g., *mail mail* for letters sent through the postal system instead of e-mail and *book book* for printed books instead of e-books.

In 1982, I observed: "From what I have been able to determine, there is no word for this phenomenon, and *'word word'* seemed to be a logical name to give it." Richard Nordquist, PhD in English, professor emeritus of rhetoric and English at Armstrong Atlantic State University, noted in his online language forum that there actually is a more formal term for a *word word*, which is the eminently forgettable: *contrastive focus reduplication*.[8] (Word word now appears in several major reference works including *The Oxford Companion to the English Language*, which suggests it has already left *contrastive focus reduplication* in the dust.)[9]

WORK IN PROGRESS. Term coined by **Ford Madox Ford** for a not-yet-complete artistic, theatrical, or musical work, often made available for public viewing or listening. Ford applied it for snippets of James Joyce's *Ulysses,* which he published as the editor of the *Transatlantic Review*. (The term is now used to describe young athletes who are raw but talented.)[10]

WORKAHOLIC. In 1971, Dr. **Wayne E. Oates** (1917-1999) wrote *Confessions of a Workaholic: The Facts about Work Addiction*, adding a word to the lexicon of the English language. His concept was that work can become an addiction, akin to alcoholism. Oates remarked in an interview at the time the book was published that the work addict "drops out of the human community" in a drive for peak performance. Oates's use of *-aholic* opened the drawbridge for a host of new words implying addictions. Although *chocoholic* and *cakeaholic* were already in use, in the wake of *workaholic*, came *shopaholic*, *computerholic*, and so on.[11]

WORLD'S MY OYSTER. In *Merry Wives of Windsor* **Shakespeare** uses the phrase "the world's mine oyster," meaning the world is the place from which to extract profit—as one would extract a pearl from an oyster.

Why then the world's mine oyster,
Which I with sword will open.[12]

WUNDERKIND. Wonder child; a highly talented child; a child prodigy, especially in music. The word was borrowed from German and introduced into English by **George Bernard Shaw** in 1891: "Every generation produces its infant Raphaels and infant Rosciuses, and Wunderkinder who can perform all the childish feats of Mozart."[13]

XYZ

x. As a verb to supply with X's in place of type or to X out. **Edgar Allan Poe** wrote in a 1849 essay entitled "X-ing a Paragrab": "'I shell have to x this ere paragrab,' said he to himself, as he read it over . . . So x it he did, unflinchingly, and to press it went x-ed."

XANTIPPE. The wife of Socrates, portrayed as a scolding and quarrelsome woman. By extension any nagging or irritable woman.

In **Shakespeare**'s *The Taming of the Shrew,* Petruchio compares Katherine "As Socrates' Xantippe or a worse" in act 1, scene 2.[1]

YAHOO. In **Jonathan Swift**'s satirical novel *Gulliver's Travels,* a *Yahoo* is one of a race of brutes, having the form and all the vices of humans, who are subject to the Houyhnhnm, an intelligent equine race: "The Fore-feet of the Yahoo differed from my Hands in nothing else, but the Length of the Nails, the Coarseness and Brownness of the Palms, and the Hairiness on the Backs." The word has become a charactronym for a boorish person or lout, and beginning in 1994, as the name of Yahoo!. com of a popular Internet server that began as a student hobby and evolved into a global brand that has changed the way people communicate with each other, find and access information, and purchase things. The name Yahoo! began as an acronym for "yet another hierarchical officious oracle," but the founders of the company insisted that they ultimately selected the name because they liked the general definition of a yahoo: "rude, unsophisticated, and uncouth"—a way they described themselves.[2]

YES MAN. The term came from a 1913 **T. A. 'Tad' Dorgan** (1877–1929) cartoon in which the *yes men* were assistant newspaper editors praising the word of the editor. Dorgan was famous as a satirical cartoonist and, later, as a sports commentator, first on the *San Francisco Bulletin* (1892–1902) and later on the *New York Journal*. New Zealand British lexicographer **Eric Partridge** (1894–1979) wrote about Dorgan in his *Dictionary of Catch Phrases*: "It was he who coined the phrases, 'Yes, we have no bananas,' '23-skiddoo,' 'See what the boys in the back room will have,' 'Officer, call a cop,' and 'Let him up, he's all cut [drunk].' Among the other apothegms he invented, still part of our common speech, were such daisies as 'The first hundred years are the hardest,' 'The only place you'll find sympathy is in the dictionary' and 'Half the world are squirrels and the other half are nuts.' Tad evolved the catch phrase 'nobody home' to denote incomprehension, witlessness, or downright idiocy in those he was shafting."[3]

YOGIBOGEYBOX. The paraphernalia of a spiritualist in **James Joyce**'s *Ulysses*.

ZARK. An all-purpose expletive created by the English humorist and science fiction novelist **Douglas Noel Adams** (1952–2001) for his internationally bestselling science fiction novel *The Hitchhiker's Guide to the Galaxy.*

ZELIG. A person who is able to befriend the influential and powerful. It is the invention of **Woody Allen** for his 1983 film of the same name whose main character, Leonard Zelig, is a nondescript man who, out of his desire to fit in and be liked, takes on the characteristics of the strong and famous personalities around him.

ZOMBIFICATION. The process by which consumerism and "soul-sapping popular culture" turns the living into the walking dead, a term coined by Romanian-born American writer and poet **Andrei Codrescu**. "The world is undergoing zombification. It was gradual for a while, a few zombies here and there, mostly in high office, where being a corpse in a suit was de rigueur . . . The worst part about zombies raging unchecked is the slow paralysis they induce in people who aren't quite zombies yet."

EPILOGUE—COLD COMFORT

There are fewer authorisms by contemporary writers in this collection than by those who died before the dawn of the twentieth century—and even fewer by contemporary women writers. This was not intentional; nor is it surprising. A large part of the explanation can be found in the competition from other fields (food, technology, pop culture to name a few) and the hurdles writers face to have their new words accepted by the public and by the official gatekeepers in the editorial offices of the *Oxford English Dictionary*, *Merriam-Webster*, and their ilk. But the fact is that the mission of these lexical guardians is not to please writers but to serve a language.

The reality is that writers occasionally attempt to get a word into play but this is easier said than done. Take for example *Sabbath gasbags*, the term coined by American writer Calvin Trillin to describe those who populate the Sunday morning television talk shows from Washington, DC. After coining the term, he embarked on a plan to systematically insinuate the phrase into the language. As he wrote of the crusade in the *New York Times*, "I first used it in a newspaper column. Then I used it in a book. Then I used it on television shows, gradually trying to drop modifiers like 'the people I refer to as.' Still nothing."

Trillin's futile quest may have had a whiff of satire about it, but it still underscored the point that it is difficult to get a word into the dictionary and doubly so if you work at it. The irony of this is that a quick check of the *OED* reveals that Trillin is listed as the first quote for two terms: the spicy *Buffalo chicken wing* (1980) and the adjective *wonky* (1978)—neither of which seem to be his. "First use" can be a bit tricky because it not only lists obvious coinages but also words that an author was the first to record—or at least the first that could be cited by the editors, which is certainly the case with Buffalo wings, a phenomenon Trillin was reporting on.

A few weeks before finishing my first draft of this book I checked with the latest online edition of the *Oxford English Dictionary* to see if either of the neologisms that I claim—*word word* or *demonym*—were listed and they were not. I checked by searching the online version of the *OED* for words for which I was given credit for having first used.

Much to my surprise I was credited with being the first to use three different words: (1) a synonym for drunk (*arseholed*), which came from a list of drunk terms I had collected in a successful attempt to get into *The Guinness Book of World Records* for the most number of synonyms ever collected for a single concept—currently at 2,985; (2) a transitive verb fashioned from the name of a common instrument of dental hygiene for the act of using said instrument *(Waterpicked)*; and (3) an eponym for nuclear recklessness based on a character developed by Terry Southern for his novel and subsequent film *Dr.*

Strangelove or: How I Learned to Stop Worrying and Love the Bomb (*Strangelovean*).

Although I would love to take credit for enriching the language, I did not create any of these three words and was nothing more than a carrier who took terms I had heard or read elsewhere and used them in print. I have made every effort in *Authorisms* to point out whether words were coined by writers or attributed to them for being the first to introduce borrowed words or popularize obscure ones.

I have not included in this collection the first use of the term *comfort food* (i.e., food that comforts or affords solace; hence, any food—often with a high sugar or carbohydrate content—that is associated with childhood or with home cooking). The phrase is attributed to food writer, crime novelist, and old friend Phyllis Richman who wrote in the *Washington Post* magazine of December 25, 1977: "Along with grits, one of the comfort foods of the South is black-eyed peas." Richman did write the passage as the *Post*'s food editor but does not believe she invented the term. Rather she insists she picked it up elsewhere.

On the other hand Richman proudly claims to have coined *elechinondros*, a verbal wild card, which means it has no intrinsic meaning—but means anything and everything. Says Richman, "I just used it wherever it sounded good, in one exam or paper in most classes I had throughout high school and college. Nobody ever questioned it."

The nonce word has not taken off, perhaps because Richman lacks the literary clout of, say, James Joyce to help her get it listed in the *OED*, which includes at least a dozen nonce words from the writings of James Joyce. Despite the success of Joyce's aforementioned *quark*, the problem with this class of words is that they have no legs (or in the case of those coined for poems, feet). *Smellsip* and *smilesmirk* are two nonce words from Joyce's *Ulysses*—the former for smelling and sipping at once and the latter for smiling in a smirking matter—which are listed in the *OED* with the single example of their use in Joyce.

Attempts to elevate nonce words to common use, let alone *OED* status, commonly result in failure. In 1948, Max J. Herzberg, editor of *Word Study*, a publication of Merriam-Webster, wrote to a number of well-known writers to ask if they had created any new words. The results were fascinating and mixed—but all but a few were then and still are today nonce words. For example, novelist Sinclair Lewis, the first American to receive the Nobel Prize in Literature, replied to the request:

> I'm the inventor of the following words—though you may decide that none of them have sufficiently caught on:
>
> *hobohemia*
>
> *philanthrobber*
>
> and, though I'm not quite sure whether I invented it or stole it:
>
> *Kiplingo.*
>
> and one that I have never yet used but shall some day, re the American ethos:
>
> *teetotalitarian*

Novelist Conrad Aiken pointed out that he had created and used the word *smubtle* in his 1927 book *Blue Voyage* on page 48 along with the noun *smubleties*. Aiken explains, "Its meaning of course is obvious enough: a combination of the smutty and the subtle." Poet Louis Untermeyer had some rare coinages including *Peter Pantheism* for a hedonistic refusal to grow up, and *Debussybodies* for American musicians who were copying and prying into the French impressionistic style.[1]

The point of all of this being that even writers with large readerships have a tough time getting their clever nonce words accepted. On the other hand, Sinclair Lewis never intended to have the name of his most famous character and the title of his most famous novel turned into a word: *Babbitt*.

Appendix: How Many Words and Phrases Did Shakespeare Actually Coin?

n 1997, while working as a consultant to the Merriam-Webster Co. of Springfield, Massachusetts, I helped to acquire and publish a book by Jeffrey McQuain and Stanley Malless entitled *Coined by Shakespeare—Words and Meanings First Penned by the Bard*. The book still reigns as the authority on Shakespearean coinage. Two lines in the introduction to the book fascinated me then as they do today: "How many words has Shakespeare added to English? Guesses have ranged from a few hundred terms to more than 10,000 with the most likely estimate approximately 1,700 words."[1]

Since that book was published in 1998, a number of new estimates have come into play that are in dazzling disagreement, including these three that appeared in print between 2006 and 2007 and are listed from high bid to low:

- "He coined nearly six thousand new words." —Seth Lerer, *Inventing English: A Portable History of the Language*[2]

- "He coined ... 2,035 words." —Bill Bryson, *Shakespeare: The World as Stage*[3]
- "His writing not only shows the richness the language had already achieved but also shows Shakespeare to have been a prolific word coiner. *Besmirch, impede, rant,* and *wild-goose chase* are a few of the more than 1,000 words and phrases that he evidently added to our language." —Barbara Wallraff, *American Scholar,* Spring 2006[4]

The World Wide Web was a wispy little toy in 1998 (the year Google came into play on September 27), but since then it has became a place where Shakespeare's name produces 87.3 million hits and where there are scores of websites devoted to honoring, examining, or dismissing him. With this has come a host of new e-estimates, all pulled from sites in late 2013:

- Mental Floss asserts that there are "over 2200 never-before-seen words" in Shakespeare's scripts and poems.
- A website entitled *No Sweat Shakespeare* claims that "in all of his work—the plays, the sonnets and the narrative poems—Shakespeare uses 17,677 words: Of those words, Shakespeare invented an incredible 1,700 of them!"[5]

The list goes on with McQuain and Malless's estimate of 1,700 words being the most common: Words Shakespeare Invented—Shakespeare Online, by Amanda Mabillard, and *Shakespeare on Toast: Getting a Taste for the Bard* by Ben Crystal.

So do we give credit to Shakespeare for way more than he deserves? Probably, especially if one looks at the math. Shakespeare's vocabulary was something on the order of 15,000 words and the only dictionary of the English language at the time of Shakespeare's death contained a mere 5,080 words.[6]

The first question that must be asked is how many of these words were simply words in common use but not recorded until Shakespeare's plays were published, such as the term *garden house,* which means house in the garden or summer house, or the word *leapfrog,* which is on just about everyone's list of Bardicisms. Near the end of *Henry V,* King Henry pledges his love to Princess Katherine of France. The king alludes to his physical dexterity by saying that "if I could win a lady at leap-frog . . . I should quickly leap into a wife," act 5, scene 2, lines 136–39. Is it not possible—or probable—that leapfrog was a common game of Shakespeare's childhood known by that name to his audience, but not yet published in English literature? If this game in which players vault over each other's stooped backs was not known to Shakespeare's Globe Theatre audience, the line and the scene would have made no sense.

Also, if Shakespeare's neologisms had been in the thousands as some have claimed, wouldn't that have been a barrier between Shakespeare and his audience—akin to staging a play today with words from Klingon or Esperanto tossed in to the dialogue?

It seems safe to conclude that Shakespeare created or introduced many less than a thousand words and phrases still in common use. This is in line with the list of words created by Shakespeare by American author and professor of biochemistry Michael Macrone's national bestseller, *Brush Up Your Shakespeare!* first published in 1990 and later expanded in 2000. Macrone is the only modern writer to actually compile a list and work to refine it over time. His most recent version of the list appeared in 2003 in the *Shakespeare Oxford Newsletter*, in which 501 words and phrases are listed.[7]

Although Macrone has found some terms that predate the *OED*, there are words on his list that have been taken away from Shakespeare in the third edition of the dictionary dated September 2007. One of these words is *puke* because of several earlier uses. Puke (along with its first cousins *barf*, *hurl*, and *upchuck*) is an onomatopoetic word that likely came out of taverns and inns where overindulgence was common. The word *zany* (the last on Macrone's list) was predated in an earlier version of the *OED*.

On the other hand, there are words that do not appear in Macrone's list and other lists that are "one-offs" that did not become part of the larger language and languish on the back burner of common speech.

Do these count?

There are those who have made a case for them. In *The Shakespeare Key* by Charles and Mary Cowden Clarke, a book published in 1879, this appeal appears:

SHAKESPEARE, with the right and might of a true poet, and with his peculiar royal privilege as king of all poets, has minted several words that deserve to become current in our language. He coined them for his own special use to express his own special meanings in his own special passages; but they are so expressive and so well framed to be exponents of certain particulars in meaning common to us all, that they deserve to become generally adopted and used.

The Clarkes nominate for general adoption:

affin'd = united by affinity
attask'd = taken to task
cadent = falling, trickling, pouring down
co-mart = joint bargains, compact made together, in the same manner that the words co-heiress, co-partner, &c.
congreeing = agreeing with itself, in all its parts
congreeted = greeted each other, met together
dispunge = discharge as from a sponge
fracted = broken
germins = the principles of germination
immoment = unmomentous, of no moment or importance
insisture = fixed position, appointed situation, steadfast place
intrenchant = incapable of being cut
mirable = wonderful, that which is to be admired at, or marvelled at

needly = needfully, necessarily

oppugnancy = warring opposition

propugnation = power of defense

roted = retained by rote; acquired by rote and held
ready for conventional utterance and

unsisting = unstill, never resting[8]

Finally, Shakespeare was able to take existing words and fashion them into other forms of speech.

As lexicographer Rob Kyff pointed out in one of his syndicated columns on words entitled "Don't Guilt People for Verbing Nouns": "William Shakespeare was the first to use 'champion' as a verb, 'scuffle' as a noun, 'hush' as an adjective ('hush money') and 'accused' as a noun ('the accused')."[9] Even if these adaptations were first made by the Bard (which they probably were not) do they count in the total?

Then there are the extended phrases—metaphors, similes, and aphorisms—which are often listed as coinages. In *Shakespeare on Toast*, Ben Crystal rattles off many of these, including: "*laughing yourself into stitches, setting your teeth on edge, not sleeping a wink, being cruel only to be kind,* and *playing fast and loose.*"[10] British comedian and sometimes Shakespearean actor Lenny Henry noted in a 2012 essay in the *Evening Standard* entitled "What Will Taught Me": "The first thing I've learned about the Bard is that you may think you're keeping him at arm's length but his phrases crop up all over the English language. Things you thought your parents had made up were actually first coined by Bill Shakestick."

Henry goes on to list a number of them beginning with the letter A: "A sorry sight"; "All corners of the world"; "All that glitters is not gold"; "As pure as the driven snow"; "At one fell swoop." He noted later in the essay that when his dad ran for the bus in the morning he would say, "Let slip the dogs of war"—a Bardism.

The question of Shakespeare's word count was put to John F. Andrews, founder and president of the Shakespeare Guild, whose lifetime of Shakespearean scholarship netted him, among other honors, the Order of the British Empire in the year 2000.

"Like you, I suspect," he wrote in reply to my query, "I'd love to think that Shakespeare introduced a good deal more than 500 of the words that remain in today's dictionaries. But since our print and manuscript records from his time, and even more from the periods that preceded it, are so scant, there is really no way of knowing."

Andrews, whose Shakespearean credits are legion, has worked on restoring Shakespeare's scripts to their earliest forms. He added this: "One thing I'd note, however, is that a good number of what may well be Bardic coinages have been obliterated by later editors, who've been emending the original quarto and folio texts almost from the outset, and particularly from the early 18th century to the present. A word such as *beguide*, for example, which appears in the 1604–5 second quarto of *Hamlet*, and which strikes me as an authentically Polonian hybrid that merges 'beguile' and 'misguide,' survives only in the small-print notes of modern editions of the plays. And, trust me, there are scores of similar instances. One of my favorites is *envie*, a form that appears in the line 'Is it for him you do envie me so?' in *The Taming of the Shrew*. Here the meter calls for a stress on the first syllable, and the context makes it clear that Bianca means 'vie with' primarily, and 'envy' in the usual sense only secondarily."[*][11]

So there it is—a number that is no easier to determine than the number of birds in a given tract of parkland on a given day at a given time.

---

* Another example of this phenomenon is pointed out in Jeffrey McQuain and Stanley Malless: "Shakespeare uses pander as a verb only once, and that use occurs in *Hamlet*. As Hamlet accuses his mother of complicity in his father's murder, he suggests that her motive was lust, by which 'reason panders will' (III.iv.88). Although the quarto editions substitute pardons, the First Folio chooses panders."

Acknowledgments

I would like to thank Tom Mann of the Library of Congress for his help with this book. Special thanks also to the staff of the Rare Books and Special Collections of the Public Library of Cincinnati and Hamilton County, which houses the Louis E. Kahn Collection of Dictionaries, which was most useful in compiling this collection. I would also like to acknowledge my indebtedness to fellow author Bill Young for his help with this book and for his pioneering work as a:

PLACOANAGRAMMIST *noun.* (/plækoʊænəgræmest/) [From the Greek *placo* (flat plate or tablet) + ana (anew) + *gram* (something written) + *ist.*] A person who develops anagrams of people's names suitable to be engraved on their tombstones as epitaphs.

I am also indebted to John F. Andrews, OBE, founder and president of the Shakespeare Guild for his advice on dealing with Shakespeare's neologic box score and to John M. Morse of Merriam-Webster for his work on coming up with the consensus term for Shakespeare's 450th. Also thanks to Rev. David Baverstock and Richard Lederer for their help in the quest for the proper term. Amatoli Etzioini, John Denis Huston, Joseph C. Goulden, Phyllis Richman, Bob Skole, and Jim Srodes.

Bibliography

Alexander, Rose. "Slang and Popular Phrases Used by Shakespeare etc." Los Angeles: Rose Alexander, 1936.

Anderson, Verily. "Common and Uncommon Words." *Shakespeare Oxford Newsletter* 39.4 (2003).

Andrewes, George. *A Dictionary of the Slang and Cant Languages: Ancient and Modern, as Used by Adam Tylers, Badgers, Bullies . . . and Every Class of Offenders.* London: George Smeeton, 1809.

Anglicus, Ducange (pseud.). *The Vulgar Tongue: Comprising Two Glossaries of Slang, Cant, and Flash Words and Phrases . . .* London: Bernard Quaritch, 1857.

Barrett, Grant. *The Official Dictionary of Unofficial English: A Crunk Omnibus for Thrillionaires and Bampots for the Ecozoic Age.* New York: McGraw-Hill, 2006.

Bradlee, Ben. *A Good Life: Newspapering and Other Adventures.* 1st Touchstone Editions. New York: Simon and Schuster, 1996.

Brown, Ivor, and John Carnegie. *Ivor Brown's Book of Words: Comprising a Word in Your Ear and Just Another Word.* London: J. Cape, 1944.

Bryson, Bill. *Shakespeare: The World as Stage.* New York: HarperCollins, Eminent Lives, 2007.

Ciardi, John. *A Browser's Dictionary, and Native's Guide to the Unknown American Language.* New York: HarperCollins, 1980.

———. *A Second Browser's Dictionary.* New York: HarperCollins, 2001.

Clarke, Charles and Mary Cowden. *The Shakespeare Key.* New York: Frederick Ungar Publishing Co., 1879.

Cousineau, Phil. *Wordcatcher: an Odyssey into the World of Weird and Wonderful Words.* Berkeley, CA: Viva Editions, 2010.

Craigie, William A., and James R. Hulbert. *A Dictionary of American English* on *Historical Principles*. 4 vols. Chicago: University of Chicago Press, 1938–44.

Crystal, Ben. *Shakespeare on Toast: Getting a Taste for the Bard.* London: Icon Books Ltd., 2010.

Cutler, Charles L. *O Brave New Words! Native American Loanwords in Current English.* Norman, OK: University of Oklahoma Press, 1994.

Dalzell, Tom. *Flappers 2 Rappers: American Youth Slang.* Dover ed. Mineola, NY: Dover Publications, 2011.

Dickson, Paul. *Words: A Connoisseur's Collection of Old and New, Weird and Wonderful Words.* New York: Delacorte Press, 1982.

———. *Words from the White House: Words and Phrases Coined or Popularized by America's Presidents.* New York: Walker and Company, 2013.

Garg, Anu. "Coining Words." *Writing!* Feb.–March 2008: S6.

Goulden, Joseph C. *The Dictionary of Espionage: Spyspeak into English.* Dover ed. Mineola, NY: Dover Publications, 2012.

Grose, Francis. *A Classical Dictionary of the Vulgar Tongue.* London: Printed for S. Hooper, 1785.

Hall, Benjamin Homer. *A Collection of College Words and Customs.* Cambridge, MA: John Bartlett, 1851.

Hargrave, Basil. *Origins and Meanings of Popular Phrases and Names Including Those Which Came into Use During the Great War.* London: T. Werner Laurie, Ltd., 1925.

Harker, E. Joseph. *Last Ever Notes and Queries.* A Guardian Book. London: Fourth Estate Ltd., 1998.

Harker, Joseph, ed. *Notes and Queries.* Vol. 5. London: Trafalgar Square, 1995.

———, ed. *Notes and Queries.* Vol. 6. A Guardian Book. London: McClelland and Stewart Ltd., 1995.

Holt, Alfred H. *Phrase Origins.* New York: Thomas Y. Crowell, 1936.

Irwin, Godfrey, ed. *American Tramp and Underworld Slang: Words and Phrases Used by Hoboes, Tramps, Migratory Workers and Those on the Fringes of Society, with Their Uses and Origins, with a Number of Tramp Songs.* With essays on the slang and the songs by Godfrey Irwin. Terminal essay on American slang in relation to English thieves' slang by Eric Partridge. New York: Sears, 1930.

James, Brenda. *The Truth Will Out: Unmasking the Real Shakespeare.* New York: Harper Perennial, 2007.

Johnson, Burges. *The Lost Art of Profanity.* Indianapolis: Bobbs-Merrill Co., 1948.

Jones, Brian Jay. *Washington Irving—An American Original.* New York: Arcade Books, 2008.

Kane, Joseph Nathan. *Famous FIRST Facts, a Record of FIRST Happenings, Discoveries and Inventions in the United States.* New York: H. W. Wilson, 1933.

————, *More First Facts*. New York: H. W. Wilson, 1935.

Kyff, Rob. "Don't Guilt People for Verbing Nouns." *Tribune-Review/ Pittsburgh Tribune-Review*, July 14, 2012.

Lerer, Seth. *Inventing English: A Portable History of the Language*. New York: Columbia University Press, 2007.

Lewis, C. S. *Studies in Words* (canto). Cambridge: Cambridge University Press, 1967.

Mabillard, Amanda. *Words Shakespeare Invented*. Shakespeare Online. Aug. 20, 2000. www.shakespeare-online.com/biography/wordsinvented.html.

Macrone, Michael. " 'Household Words': Common and Uncommon Words Coined by Shakespeare ... an Excerpt from *Brush Up Your Shakespeare!*" *Shakespeare Oxford Newsletter* 39.1 (2003): 10.

————. " 'Household Words': Common and Uncommon Words Coined by Shakespeare, Part II." *Shakespeare Oxford Newsletter* 39.2 (2003): 10.

McQuain, Jeffrey, and Stanley Malless. *Coined by Shakespeare: Words and Meanings First Penned by the Bard*. Springfield, MA: Merriam-Webster, 1998.

Mathews, Mitford M. *American Words*. Cleveland: World Publishing, 1959.

Mead, Leon. *How Words Grow: A Brief Study of Literary Style, Slang, and Provincialisms*. New York: T. Y. Crowell and Co., 1907.

Mencken, Henry L. *The American Language*, fourth ed., New York: (1945).

————. *The American Language, Supplement I*, New York: (1945).

Merriam-Webster. *Word Study*. Vols. 1–45 (Sept. 1925–Oct. 1969).

Meyer, Graham. "Top 40 Chicago Words—Our Contributions to the English Language." *Chicago*, July 2010.

Morris, Evan. *The Word Detective*. Chapel Hill, NC: Algonquin Books, 2000.

Morris, William, and Mary. *Morris Dictionary of Word and Phrase Origins*. New York: Collins Reference, 1988.

Plotnik, Arthur. "Shall We Coin a Term? When No Other Word Will Do, Maybe a Neologism Will." *Writer*, Dec. 2003.

————. *Spunk and Bite: A Writer's Guide to Bold, Contemporary Style*. New York: Random House Reference, 2007.

Pollin, Burton R. "Poe, Creator of Words." Baltimore: Edgar Allan Poe Society of Baltimore, 1974. This lecture was delivered by Dr. Pollin at the Fifty-first Annual Commemoration Program of the Poe Society, October 7, 1973. The Word List from this lecture is available online at www.eapoe.org/papers/psblctrs/pl19741s.htm.

Pratte, Alf. "A Word on Wordsmiths." *Masthead*, Spring 1999.

Pyles, Thomas. *Words and Ways of American English*. New York: Random House, 1952.

Read, Allen Walker. *Milestones in the History of English in America*. Ed. Richard W. Bailey. Durham, NC: Duke University Press Books, 2002.

Reid, Alastair. *Ounce, Dice, Trice.* New York: NYR Children's Collection, 2009.

Saussy, George Stone III. *The Oxter English Dictionary: Uncommon Words Used by Uncommonly Good Writers.* New York: Facts on File Inc., 1985.

Shenker, Israel. *Harmless Drudges: Wizards of Language—Ancient, Medieval and Modern.* Bronxville, NY: Barnhart Books, 1979.

Smith, C. Alphonso. *New Words Self-Defined.* New York: Doubleday, Page & Co., 1919.

Smith, Mrs. Chetwood. *History's Most Famous Words.* Boston: Lothrup, Lee and Shepard, Co., 1926.

Steinmetz, Sol. *Semantic Antics: How and Why Words Change Meaning.* New York: Random House Reference, 2008.

———. *There's a Word for It.* New York: Harmony Books, 2010.

Stoopnagle, Colonel Lemuel Q. *You Wouldn't Know Me from Adam.* New York: Whittlesey House, 1944.

Waldhorn, Arthur. *Concise Dictionary of the American Language.* New York: Philosophical Library, 1956.

Wallraff, Barbara. *Word Fugitives.* New York: HarperCollins, 2006.

Webber, Elizabeth, and Mike Feinsilber. *Grand Allusions A Lively Guide to Those Expressions, Terms and References You Ought to Know but Might Not.* Washington, DC: Farragut Pub. Co., 1990.

Wilson, Edward O. *Biophilia.* Cambridge: Harvard University Press, 1984.

Wordsworth, Dot. "Dickens's Coinages." *Spectator,* Feb. 18, 2012: 62.

Notes

INTRODUCTION

1. Arthur Plotnik, "Shall We Coin a Term? When No Other Word Will Do, Maybe a Neologism Will," *Writer*, Dec. 2003.
2. Logan Pearsall Smith, *Milton and His Modern Critics* (Oxford: Oxford University Press, 1940), 54.
3. *Guardian*, Jan. 27, 2008, A-3.
4. Ben Crystal, *Shakespeare on Toast: Getting a Taste for the Bard* (London: Icon Books Ltd., 2010), 11.
5. Brenda James, *The Truth Will Out: Unmasking the Real Shakespeare* (New York: Harper Perennial, 2007), 7.
6. "[W]hen I happened to be writing about lacrosse in Manchester, England, I worked in the word 'Mancunian' three times in one short paragraph. It was the second-best demonym I'd ever heard, almost matching Vallisoletano (a citizen of Valladolid). The planet, of course, is covered with demonyms, and after scouring the world in conversations on this topic with Mary Norris I began a severely selective, highly subjective A-list, extending Mancunian and Vallisoletano through thirty-five others at this writing, including Wulfrunian (Wolverhampton), Novocastrian (Newcastle), Trifluvian (Trois-Rivières), Leodensian (Leeds), Minneapolitan (Minneapolis), Hartlepudlian (Hartlepool), Liverpudlian (you knew it), Haligonian (Halifax), Varsovian (Warsaw), Providentian (Providence), and Tridentine (Trent)." John McPhee, "Draft No. 4," *New Yorker*, April 29, 2013.
7. Leon Mead, *How Words Grow* (New York : T. Y. Crowell and Co., 1907), 181. Twain's letter to Mead was in October 1900.
8. Ibid., 179.

A

1. A discussion of this term appears in E. Joseph Harker, *Last Ever Notes and Queries*, A Guardian Book (London: Fourth Estate Ltd., 1998), 126–27. It references the Steinbeck quote as p. 206 of the Penguin edition of *Grapes of Wrath*.

2. Elizabeth Webber and Mike Feinsilber, *Grand Allusions: A Lively Guide to Those Expressions, Terms and References You Ought to Know but Might Not* (Washington, DC: Farragut Pub. Co., 1990), 8–9. Contains examples of the term in use. An annotated version of the original by Jack Lynch of Rutgers University can be seen at http://andromeda.rutgers.edu/~jlynch/Texts/modest.html.

3. E. Sitwell, *Coll. Poems* (1930) 124: Shone . . . apricots so ripe their kernels seem Gemmed amethysts,—the rose abricotine,

4. *Oxford English Dictionary*, 1906 'O. Henry' Four Million (1916) 14. The financial loss of a dollar sixty-five, all so far fulfilled according to Hoyle.

5. Alf Pratte, "A Word on Wordsmiths," *Masthead*, Spring 1999.

6. Ellen Goodman, "With Age Comes Wisdom—We Can Only Hope," *Columbia Daily Tribune*, April 1, 2008.

7. William Rose Benét, ed., *The Reader's Encyclopedia: An Encyclopedia of World Literature and the Arts* (New York: Thomas Y. Crowell, 1948), 15.

8. Lawrence E. Cole, *General Psychology* (New York: McGraw-Hill, 1939), 520, 586.

9. Redgate, "The Red Pencil," *Washington Post*, March 17, 1998, D19.

10. *Oxford English Dictionary*, 1836 W. Irving, *N.Y. Mirror* 4 Nov. 145/2: "The almighty dollar, that great object of universal devotion throughout our land."

11. *Oxford English Dictionary*, G. H. Lewes, "Contemporary Literature of France," *Westminster Review* 58 (Oct. 1852): 614–30. 1842 *N.Y. Rev.* Jan. 167.

12. Isaac Goldberg, *The Wonder of Words: An Introduction to Language for Everyman* (New York: D. Appleton-Century, 1938), 246.

13. *Oxford English Dictionary*, 1838 J. F. Cooper, *Home as Found* I. vi. 93.

14. Leon Mead, *How Words Grow* (New York: T. Y. Crowell and Co., 1907), 105.

15. Elizabeth Webber and Mike Feinsilber, *Grand Allusions: A Lively Guide to Those Expressions, Terms and References You Ought to Know but Might Not* (Washington, DC: Farragut Pub. Co., 1990), 21.

16. *Oxford English Dictionary*, 1920 G. Ade, *Hand-made Fables*, 83.

17. *Oxford English Dictionary*, Shakespeare, *Macbeth* (1623) i. vii. 2.

18. *Oxford English Dictionary*, 1887 tr. J. Verne, *Clipper of the Clouds* iv. 36.

B

1. Elizabeth Webber and Mike Feinsilber, *Grand Allusions: A Lively Guide to Those Expressions, Terms and References You Ought to Know but Might Not* (Washington, DC: Farragut Pub. Co., 1990), 27.

2. Alfred Holt, *Phrase Origins* (New York: Thomas Y. Crowell, 1936),10.
3. O. Henry, *Cabbages and Kings* (New York: Doubleday, Page and Co.,1904).
4. John Soluri, *Banana Cultures: Agriculture, Consumption, and Environmental Change in Honduras and the United States* (Austin, TX: University of Texas Press, 2005), 2.
5. *Oxford English Dictionary*, 1901   G. B. Shaw, *Three Plays for Puritans* Pref. p. xxxi. 1903   G. B. Shaw, *Man & Superman* Ep. Ded. 30   Foolish Bardolaters make a virtue of this after their fashion.
6. This information appears in an article about David Block in the online sports magazine *Grantland*: http://www.grantland.com/story/_/ id/9681627/baseball-archaeologist-david-block.
7. *Oxford English Dictionary*, 1958   J. C. Holmes in *Esquire*, Feb. 35/2.
8. Ann Charters, *Kerouac: A Biography* (New York: St. Martin's Griffin), 1994.
9. Quoted in Andrew Sinclair, *The Better Half: The Emancipation of the American Woman* (New York: Praeger,1965), ix.
10. Jeffrey D. Schultz, John G. West, and Iain Maclean, eds., *Encyclopedia of Religion in American Politics* (Phoenix: Oryx, 1999), 25.
11. Julie L. Thomas, "Sanger, Margaret 1879–1966," in *Encyclopedia of Sex and Gender*, vol. 4, ed. Fedwa Malti-Douglas (Detroit: Macmillan Reference USA, 2007), 1298–1300.
12. Elizabeth Webber and Mike Feinsilber, *Grand Allusions: A Lively Guide to Those Expressions, Terms and References You Ought to Know but Might Not* (Washington, DC: Farragut Pub. Co., 1990), 45. *Oxford English Dictionary*, 1906   W. James Let. 11 Sept. (1920) II. 26.
13. William Rose Benét, ed., *The Reader's Encyclopedia: An Encyclopedia of World Literature and the Arts* (New York: Thomas Y. Crowell, 1948), 116.
14. "Coined the Word Boom," *Boston Globe*, Jan. 1, 1897, 2. The *Oxford English Dictionary* shows a later citation listed as the earliest use: 1879 *Lumberman's Gaz.*, 19 Dec., "There has not been the boom upon lumber experienced in many other articles of merchandise."
15. *Oxford English Dictionary*, 1667   J. Evelyn, *Mem.* (1857) III. 161.   We have hardly any words that do . . . fully express the French naïveté, ennui, bizarre, etc.
16. Max J. Herzbergs ed., "Brain-washing" in *Word Study* 2043, no. 1 (April 1953): 4. G. & C. Merriam Company, Springfield, MA.

C

1. *Oxford English Dictionary*, 1934   A. Huxley, *Beyond Mexique Bay*, 18. A Calypso Tent . . . is . . . a tin roof on posts—in which..the local talent assembles to rehearse certain songs composed against the coming of Carnival. 1934 A. Huxley, *Beyond Mexique Bay*, 19.

2. *Oxford English Dictionary,* 1921 G. B. Si Iayv, *Pen Portraits* (1932), 262. The Chaplinesque invention of Simon of Nantua.
3. *Oxford English Dictionary,* 1851 'G. Eliot' *Letters* 18 Sept. (1954) vol. 1.
4. Barbara Brynko, "Wikinomics: The Crossroads of Collaboration," *Information Today,* April 2007, 31.
5. www.bbc.co.uk/news/magazine-21956748.
6. *New York Times Magazine,* July 14, 1996, SM31.

D

1. Alf Pratte, "A Word on Wordsmiths," *Masthead,* Spring 1999.
2. Robert Van Gelder, *New York Times,* October 19, 1941, BR2.
3. C. S. Lewis, *Studies in Words* (Cambridge: Cambridge University Press, 1967), 268.
4. From Owen's "Report on British Fossil Reptiles," part 2. *Report of the British Association for the Advancement of Science* (Plymouth, England: 1842).
5. Swift, *Let. to Pope* 22 Apr. in *Lett. Dr. Swift* (1741) 224 [Cf. ib. 143 (1737). [A long fit of deafness hath unqualified me for conversing.]
6. *Oxford English Dictionary,* 1922 J. Joyce, *Ulysses* ii. 491.
7. *Chicago Tribune,* October 29, 1938, 14.

E

1. *Oxford English Dictionary,* 1917 R. W. Lardner, *Gullible's Trav.* 27, "I and my Missus and Mrs. Hatch clubbed together on the straps and I got a earful o' the real dope."
2. Rachel Shteir, *Striptease: The Untold History of the Girlie Show* (New York: Oxford University Press, 2004), 216.
3. Frank Worbs, "A New Word Is Coined," *Beaver Valley Times,* February 17, 1972.
4. *Oxford English Dictionary,* 1883 R. L. Stevenson, *Treasure of Franchard* vi. He uses it [the word *ratiocinate*] . . . in the sense of *to ergotise,* implying as it were . . . a vein of sophistry.
5. See www.phrases.org.uk/meanings/phrases-sayings-shakespeare.html. This web page contains detailed information on 135 phrases from Shakespeare. There is no sourcing beyond the page itself.
6. *Oxford English Dictionary,* 1944 J. R. R. Tolkien *Let.* 7–8 Nov. (1995) 100. For it I coined the word "eucatastrophe": the sudden happy turn in a story which pierces you with a joy that brings tears. 1947 J. R. R. Tolkien, *On Fairy Stories* in *Ess. presented to Charles Williams* ii.
7. Leon Mead, *How Words Grow* (New York: T. Y. Crowell and Co., 1907), 68.

8. "The Rusty Shed Company; Shakespeare Lovers' Fury at 'Monstrosity' That Will Stage Plays While Theatre Is Rebuilt," *Mail on Sunday*, London, England, January 23, 2005.

F

1. www.theatlantic.com/entertainment/archive/2013/04/i-apologize-for -inventing-the-word-fashionista-20-years-ago/275048.
2. *Oxford English Dictionary*, 1873 G. Vandenhoff tr. A. Dumas Man-woman 64.
3. Boyd Tonkin, "Voice of the Beat Generation Nears the End with Serenity," *Independent*, London, England, April 5, 1997.
4. *Ivanhoe*, by Sir Walter Scott, 1819. *Free*, of course, means "unbound," not "without cost." Quoted from World Wide Words, copyright Michael Quinion, 1996–2013.
5. Charles and Mary Cowden Clarke, *The Shakespeare Key* (New York: Frederick Ungar Publishing Co., 1879), 54.
6. *Oxford English Dictionary*, 1766 O. Goldsmith, *Vicar of Wakefield* I. xi. 104.

G

1. Ernst Mayr, *The Growth of Biological Thought: Diversity, Evolution, and Inheritance* (Cambridge, MA: Belknap Press, 1982), 782.
2. Marshall McLuhan, *Understanding Media: the Extensions of Man*, 1st ed. (Cambridge, MA: The MIT Press, 1994), 6.
3. Barnaby J. Feder, "Theodore Levitt, 81; Coined the Term 'Globalization,'" *New York Times*, July 6, 2006.
4. *Oxford English Dictionary*, 1944 M. Maverick in *New York Times Magazine* 21 (May 11): 1.
5. E-mail from Tom Dalzell, June 13, 2013, *Oxford English Dictionary*, *Fear and Loathing in Las Vegas*, 80, 1971.
6. Irving L. Janis, *Victims of Groupthink* (New York: Houghton Mifflin, 1972). Irving L. Janis, *Groupthink: Psychological Studies of Policy Decisions and Fiascoes*, second ed. (New York: Houghton Mifflin, 1982).

H

1. *Oxford English Dictionary*, 1836 *Last of Mohicans* II. xvi. W. Irving *Astoria* (1849) 249. "They will see the happy hunting-grounds, with the souls of the brave and good living in tents in green meadows." Charles L. Cutler,

O Brave New Words! Native American Loanwords in Current English
(Norman, OK: University of Oklahoma Press, 1994), 132.

2. *Oxford English Dictionary,* 1886 'M. Twain' *Speeches* (1923) 137.

3. Deanna R. Adams, *Rock 'n' Roll and the Cleveland Connection* (Kent, OH: Kent State University Press, 2002), 446. www.questia.com/read/109691790.

4. *Oxford English Dictionary,* 1923 W. De Beck in *N.Y. American* 26 (Oct. 9), 3.

5. *Oxford English Dictionary,* 1974 "J. le Carré," *Tinker, Tailor* vi, 48.

6. Aoife Bannon makes this assertion in his "THINK you're a real brainbox?" column in the *Sun*, London, England, May 15, 2012.

7. *Oxford English Dictionary,* 1858 O. W. Holmes, *Autocrat of Breakfast-table* vi. 143.

8. *Oxford English Dictionary,* 1839 E. A. Poe Wks. (1884) I. 132. An evidently restrained hysteria in his whole demeanor.

I

1. *Oxford English Dictionary,* 1954 *Jrnl. Amer. Psychoanal. Assoc.* 2: 327. [Report of presentation by Erik H. Erikson] George Bernard Shaw arranged for himself a psycho-social moratorium at the age of twenty when his identity crisis led him to leave . . . his family, friends and familiar work.

2. Kevin Jackson, "ARTS: A Treasury of Wit: The Victorian Art Critic John Ruskin Denounced the Excesses of Capitalism in His Essay Collection 'Unto This Last.' Kevin Jackson Explains Why He and the Cartoonist Hunt Emerson Have Turned This Message into a Comic Book," *Independent*, London, England, November 29, 2005.

3. Alf Pratte, "A Word on Wordsmiths," *Masthead*, Spring 1999, www.questia.com/read/1G1-54422419.

4. "Curtains," *New York Times Book Review*, Jan. 6, 2013.

5. Charles and Mary Cowden Clarke, *The Shakespeare Key* (New York: Frederick Ungar Publishing Co., 1879), 57.

J

1. Martyn Bone, "Jazz Age," in *Dictionary of American History*, ed. Stanley I. Kutler, third ed., vol. 4 (New York: Charles Scribner's Sons, 2003), 469–70.

2. *American Speech,* 38, 169. In 1972, *Time* magazine reported that the elementary geology course popular for athletes at the University of Pennsylvania was called Rocks for Jocks.

3. Anthony Burgess, "Here's a Dictionary You Can believe In," *Washington Times*, March 27, 1989, E1–2.

K

1. Verily Anderson, "Common and Uncommon Words," *Shakespeare Oxford Newsletter*, 39.4 (2003). Here I am quoting from the two-volume, 2,475-page *Shorter Oxford Dictionary of Historical Principals* (UK: Clarendon Press), which was revised and edited in 1933 by the highly regarded academic, C. T. Onions, Fellow of Magdalen College, Oxford, Reader of English Philology in the University of Oxford.
2. Merriam-Webster, *Word Study*, October 1948, ed. Max J. Herzberg, "Who Makes Up the New Words?" pp. 1-4, vol. 24, no. 1. G. & C. Merriam Company, Springfield, MA, p. 6.

L

1. Jeffrey McQuain and Stanley Malless, *Coined by Shakespeare: Words and Meanings First Penned by the Bard* (Springfield, MA: Merriam-Webster, 1998), 127–28.
2. Alf Pratte, "A Word on Wordsmiths," *Masthead*, Spring 1999.
3. Her obituary in the *Baltimore Sun*, February 27, 1979, A13.
4. *Life*, May 14, 1956, 91.

M

1. *Oxford English Dictionary*, "G. Eliot" in J. W. Cross, *George Eliot's Life* (1885) II. 263.
2. "The Me Decade," in *American Decades*, Gale Virtual Reference Library, ed. Judith S. Baughman et al., vol. 8: 1970–1979 (Detroit: Gale, 2001).
3. Peter D. Salins, *Assimilation, American Style* (New York: Basic Books, 1997), 10. www.questia.com/read/43129338.
4. Lawrence Lockridge, *The Ethics of Romanticism*, Cambridge University Press, Nov. 2, 1989, p. 382, where he cites vol. 7 of Byron's Letters.
5. Alf Pratte, "A Word on Wordsmiths," *Masthead*, Spring 1999.
6. The first and only citation for this nonce word in the *OED*, 1916 R. Frost *Let.* 24 May in *Lett. to L. Untermeyer* (1964), 34: Moanism and swounding. On larruping an emotion. Men's tears tragic, women's a nuisance.
7. *Oxford English Dictionary*, 1737 Swift *Let. to Pope* 23 July in *Lett. Dr. Swift* (1741).
8. *Oxford English Dictionary*, J. le Carré, *Tinker, Tailor* viii. 62, Joseph C. Goulden, *The Dictionary of Espionage: Spyspeak into English*, Dover ed. (Mineola, NY: Dover Publications, 2012), x–xl.
9. Andy Duncan, "The Humanism of C. M. Kornbluth's [The Marching Morons]," in *Flashes of the Fantastic: Selected Essays from the War of the*

Worlds Centennial: Nineteenth International Conference on the Fantastic in the Arts, ed. David Ketterer (Westport, CT: Greenwood Press, 2001), 98.

10. Nexis search: 1999, *Computer Weekly* (2 Sept.) "Our new senior DBA starts on Monday. She's a muggle. No IT background, understanding or aptitude at all."

11. "J. K. Rowling and the Billion-Dollar Empire," *Forbes*, Feb. 26, 2004.

12. *Oxford English Dictionary*, 1838 J. F. Cooper, *Homeward Bound* II. vi. 109.

13. *Oxford English Dictionary*, E. E. Cummings *Let.* 4 June (1969) 26.

N

1. P. Stockwell, "Encyclopedia of Language & Linguistics," vol. 6 (Boston: Elsevier, 2006), 5.

2. *Oxford English Dictionary*, 1883 O. Wilde in *South. Times* 6 Oct. 4/2. The nasalism of the modern American had been retained from the Puritan Fathers.

3. *Oxford English Dictionary*, 1964 I. Fleming, *You only live Twice*, x. 126.

O

1. *Oxford English Dictionary*, Thackeray, *Pendennis* (1850) I. xxix. 286.

2. *Oxford English Dictionary*, 1931 H. Crane *Let.* 21 Sept. (1965) 381; the explanation of Oz for Australia is from the *Times of India*, Oct. 8, 2006.

P

1. *Daily Telegraph*, Sydney, New South Wales, Australia, Nov. 7, 2012.

2. From "Le Collectionneur de Timbres-poste," Nov. 15, 1864; there is a discussion of the distinction between a philatelist and a stamp collector in the *Chicago Tribune* of September 18, 1932, in that the term philatelist is reserved for the advanced collector.

3. B. Jonson, *New Inne* iii. ii. 238. "Most Socratick Lady! Or, if you will Ironick! gi' you ioy O' you Platonick loue here."

4. 1913 E. H. Porter, *Pollyanna* xv, 148.

5. *Boston Globe*, June 9, 2013.

6. *c*1740 in P. Egan, *Boxiana* (1823) I. 44: "Buckhorse, and several other *Pugilists*, will shew the Art of Boxing."

7. *Oxford English Dictionary*, 1922 H. Lofting, *Doctor Dolittle* x. 92.

Q

1. Robert Stockwell and Donka Minkova, *English Words: History and Structure* (Cambridge, England: Cambridge University Press, 2001), 5.
2. 1718 N. Amhurst, *Protestant Popery* iv. 61.

R

1. Ben Bradlee, *A Good Life: Newspapering and Other Adventures*, 1st Touchstone ed. (New York: Simon and Schuster, 1996), 429.

S

1. Barry Moser, *Word Mysteries and Histories: From Quiche to Humble Pie* (Boston: Houghton Mifflin), 217–18.
2. Merriam-Webster *Word Study*, December 1948, editor Max J. Herzberg, "Invention of 'Scientist,'" page 4, vol. 24, no. 2. G. & C. Merriam Company, Springfield, MA.
3. Rachel Bowlby, *Freudian Mythologies: Greek Tragedy and Modern Identities* (New York: Oxford University Press, 2007), 32.
4. *Oxford English Dictionary, Casino Royale*, chap. 7: Rouge et Noir[6].
5. *Oxford English Dictionary*, 1959 W. Howells, *Mankind in the Making* vi. 97.
6. *Oxford English Dictionary*, 1927 S. Lewis, *Elmer Gantry* ix. 134.
7. Charles and Mary Cowden Clarke, *The Shakespeare Key* (New York: Frederick Ungar Publishing Co., 1879), 54.
8. H. L. Mencken, *The Bathtub Hoax, and Other Blasts and Bravos from the Chicago Tribune*, ed. Robert McHugh (New York: Alfred A. Knopf, 1958), 203.
9. For instance the *Ohio Repository*, May 1837: "One man, in Franklin County has lately realized thirty thousand dollars, in a speculation on slaves, which he bought in Virginia, and sold down the river."
10. Tom Vitale, "John Milton, 400 Years of 'Justifying God to Man,'" the radio program *All Things Considered*, December 7, 2008.
11. *Oxford English Dictionary*, 1933 J. R. R. Tolkien *Let.* 16 Mar. (MS.). I have actually been presented by a well-wishing old gentleman with a complete N.E.D., to my staggerment, as I had quite given up hope of possessing one. 1937 J. R. R. Tolkien, *Hobbit* xii. 221. "To say that Bilbo's breath was taken away is no description at all. There are no words left to express his staggerment."
12. *Oxford English Dictionary*, 1922 W. Lippman, *Public Opinion* vi. 93.
13. *Oxford English Dictionary*, 1913 W. Cather, *O Pioneers!* ii. vii. 144.

14. *Oxford English Dictionary Ulysses*, 530.
15. Andrei Codrescu, *The Posthuman Dada Guide: Tzara and Lenin Play Chess* (Princeton, NJ: Princeton University Press, 2009), 76.

T

1. *Oxford English Dictionary*, F. Scott Fitzgerald, *This Side of Paradise* i. 25.
2. *Oxford English Dictionary*, Reprint of the London, 1771 ed., 1967. Amsterdam: N. Israel. J. Cook *Jrnl.* 15 June (1967) III. i. 129. James Cook, *A Journal of a Voyage Round the World in H.M.S. Endeavour 1768–1771.*
3. Elizabeth Webber and Mike Feinsilber, *Grand Allusions: A Lively Guide to Those Expressions, Terms and References You Ought to Know but Might Not* (Washington, DC: Farragut Pub. Co., 1990), 342.
4. James Fenimore Cooper "Sketches of Naval Men: Edward Preble," *Graham's Magazine*, 27:205), 1845. "The Right Stuff" is discussed in the article "What Is 'The Right Stuff?' Name for Space Heroism Has Become Part of American Lexicon," *Daily Press*, Newport News, VA, May 10, 2003, D-1.
5. Alf Pratte, "A Word on Wordsmiths," *Masthead*, Spring 1999.
6. *Oxford English Dictionary*, 1897 L. Hearn, *Gleanings in Buddha-Fields* i. 24.
7. *Oxford English Dictionary*, 1749 H. Fielding, *Tom Jones* III. VIII. vii. 195. David Sano, "Twitter Creator Jack Dorsey Illuminates the Site's Founding Document." *Los Angeles Times*, February 18, 2009

U

1. Elizabeth Webber and Mike Feinsilber, *Grand Allusions: A Lively Guide to Those Expressions, Terms and References You Ought to Know but Might Not* (Washington, DC: Farragut Pub. Co., 1990), 358–59.
2. *Oxford English Dictionary*, 1871 L. Carroll *Through Looking-Glass* vi. 122.
3. *Oxford English Dictionary*, 1816 S. T. Coleridge, *Christabel* ii. 43. 1860 O. W. Holmes, *Elsie Venner* xxvi (1861), 302.
4. Alf Pratte, "A Word on Wordsmiths," *Masthead*, Spring 1999.
5. Reported in Merriam-Webster, *Word Study*, February, 1935, 1.
6. *Oxford English Dictionary*, 1947 R. Chandler *Let.* 5 Jan. in *R. Chandler Speaking* (1966) 66.

V

1. *Oxford English Dictionary*, 1918 V. Woolf, *Diary* 3 Nov. (1977) I. 213. Emphie vagulates in & out of the room.

2. E-mail from Richard Lederer of June 5, 2013.
3. *Oxford English Dictionary*, 1936 C. S. Lewis, *Allegory of Love* ii. 45.

W

1. *Oxford English Dictionary*, 1826 J. F. Cooper, *The Last of the Mohicans* II. vi. 108. Also, Charles L. Cutler, *O Brave New Words! Native American Loanwords in Current English* (Norman, OK: University of Oklahoma Press, 1994), 131.
2. *New York Times*, Aug. 20, 1996, B-6.
3. Elmer Plischke, *U.S. Department of State: A Reference History* (Westport, CT: Greenwood Press, 1999).
4. *Oxford English Dictionary, Life & Labor Bull.* 1/1.
5. Donald H. Dyal, *Historical Dictionary of the Spanish American War*, ed. Brian B. Carpenter and Mark A. Thomas (Westport, CT: Greenwood Press, 1996), 349.
6. Joseph Harker, ed., *Notes and Queries* (London: Trafalgar Square, 1995), 67; G. Ade, *Hand-made Fables*, (1920) 97: "Next day he sought out the dejected Wimp."
7. *Oxford English Dictionary, Don Juan: Canto II* clxxviii. 208.
8. See "Contrastive Focus Reduplication in English (The Salad-Salad Paper)," by Jila Ghomeshi, Ray Jackendoff, Nicole Rosen, and Kevin Russell, *Natural Language and Linguistic Theory* 22 (2004). Norquist column on Word Word = http://grammar.about.com/od/tz/g/Word-Word.htm. An example of a *word word* that came from Professor Nordquist's column was this that he collected from an online cooking forum: "Sorry for the confusion. I meant *pot pot*. Not cooking in a pot, but with pot."
9. *The Oxford Companion to the English Language* (New York: Oxford University Press, 1992), 1127.
10. Tim Haigh, "Mr. Hueffer and Mrs. Ford," *Independent*, London, England, February 25, 1996.
11. Martin, Douglas, "Wayne E. Oates, 82, Is Dead; Coined the Term 'Workaholic,'" *New York Times*, Oct. 26, 1999.
12. Joseph Harker, ed., *Notes and Queries*, a Guardian Book, vol. 6 (London: McClelland and Stewart Ltd., 1995), 41.
13. *Oxford English Dictionary* 1891 G. B. Shaw in World 23 Dec. 15/2.

X Y Z

1. Jeffrey McQuain and Stanley Malless, *Coined by Shakespeare: Words and Meanings First Penned by the Bard* (Springfield, MA: Merriam-Webster, 1998), 260.

2. As cited in *OED*: 1726 Swift, *Gulliver* II. iv. ii. 23: "The Fore-feet of the Yahoo differed from my Hands in nothing else, but the Length of the Nails, the Coarseness and Brownness of the Palms, and the Hairiness on the Backs."
3. Eric Partridge, *A Dictionary of Catch Phrases, American and British, from the Sixteenth Century to the Present Day*, rev. ed. (New York: Stein & Day Pub., 1986).

EPILOGUE

1. *Word Study*, October 1948, ed. Max J. Herzberg, "Who Makes Up the New Words?" 1–4. G. & C. Merriam Company, Springfield, MA.

APPENDIX

1. Jeffrey McQuain and Stanley Malless, *Coined by Shakespeare: Words and Meanings First Penned by the Bard* (Springfield, MA: Merriam-Webster, 1998), viii.
2. Seth Lerer, *Inventing English: A Portable History of the Language* (New York: Columbia University Press, 2007), 129.
3. Bill Bryson, *Shakespeare: The World as Stage* (New York: HarperCollins, 2007), 113.
4. http://theamericanscholar.org/shouldnt-there-be-a-word/#. UbeYcdhzxIE.
5. http://mentalfloss.com/article/48657/20-words-we-owe-william -shakespeare#ixzz2ShSXVJSe.
6. Leon Mead, *How Words Grow* (New York: T. Y. Crowell and Co., 1907), 234.
7. Michael Macrone, "'Household Words': Common and Uncommon Words Coined by Shakespeare, Part II," *Shakespeare Oxford Newsletter* 39.2 (2003): 10. American author and professor of biochemistry at Boston University, Macrone's list can be found at www.phrases.org.uk /meanings/phrases-sayings-shakespeare.html.
8. Charles and Mary Cowden Clarke, *The Shakespeare Key* (New York: Frederick Ungar Publishing Co., 1879), 54–67.
9. Rob Kyff, "Don't Guilt People for Verbing Nouns," *Tribune-Review /Pittsburgh Tribune-Review*, July 14, 2012.
10. Ben Crystal, *Shakespeare on Toast: Getting a Taste for the Bard* (London: Icon Books Ltd., 2010).
11. E-mail from John Andrews to the author, June 11, 2013. This theme is discussed in detail in John F. Andrews in *Shakespearean Illuminations: Essays in Honor of Marvin Rosenberg*, ed. Jay L. Halio and Hugh Richmond (Newark: University of Delaware Press, and London: Associated University Presses, 1998), 183–202.

Index

to the manner born, 167–68
much ado about nothing, 117
neologisms of, 4–6
one fell swoop, 126–27
salad days, 146
smilet, 152
star-cross'd, 156
what is past is prologue, 180
world's my oyster, 184
Xantippe, 185
Shapiro, Fred, 94
Sharpe, Evelyn, 182
Shaw, George Bernard, 28, 45–46, 48, 89,
    153, 184, 216n1(I)
Shelley, Mary, 72–73
Sheridan, Richard Brinsley, 107
Sherk, Bill, 34
Sinclair, Upton, 180–81
Sitwell, Edith, 16
Smith, H. Allen, 105
Smith, Logan Pearsall, 3–4, 112
Smith, Red, 177
Snowden, Ethel, 94
Soluri, John, 28
Sothern, Georgia, 61
Southern, Terry, 191–92
Spencer, Sir Charles (Charlie Chaplin),
    45–46
Spencer, Herbert, 159
Spenser, Edmund, 35
Steinbeck, John, 15, 33
Stein, Gertrude, 104
Stevenson, Adlai, 64, 77
Stevenson, Robert Louis, 65, 96–97
Stoker, Bram, 57
Stowe, Harriet Beecher, 153–54
Swift, Jonathan, 15–16, 40, 56, 103, 113,
    185–86, 222n2(XYZ)
Swope, Herbert Bayard, 48

T
Thackeray, William Makepeace, 39–40,
    127, 153, 164
Thompson, Hunter S., 80–81
Thoreau, Henry David, 46
Thurber, James, 26, 124, 132, 174,
    178–79
Times of London, 180
Toffler, Alvin, 75, 137
Tolkien, J. R. R., 66, 156, 215n6(E),
    220n11
Toynbee, Arnold, 135–36
Trillin, Calvin, 191–92
Twain, Mark, 9, 10, 78, 86–87

U
Untermeyer, Louis, 195
Uris, Leon, 44

V
Vandenhoff, G., 70
Veblen, Thorstein, 49
Verne, Jules, 24
Vonnegut, Kurt, 72, 83–84, 154

W
Waldhorn, Arthur, 118n
Wallace, Amy, 151
Wallace, Irving, 151
Wallechinsky, David, 151
Wallraff, Barbara, 198
Walpole, Horace, 148–49
Wanniski, Jude, 158
Warner, Charles Dudley, 78
Waugh, Evelyn, 108
Weber, Max, 137
Webster, H. T., 111–12
Weingarten, Gene, 23, 82–83, 138
Wheeler, John A., 33–34
Whewell, Rev. William, 147
White, William Allen, 145
Whitman, Walt, 65
Whyte, William H., 136
Winchell, Walter, 76
Wilde, Oscar, 41, 120, 218n2(N)
Williams, Meredith G., 26
Williams, Robert L., 60–61
Williams, Tennessee, 124
Wilson, E. O., 32
Wilson, Robert Anton, 71
Wilson, Sloan, 136
Winchell, Walter, 74, 93
Winfrey, Oprah, 17–18
Wister, Owen, 107
Wodehouse, P. G., 85, 102–3, 132
Wolfe, Tom, 24, 108–9, 132, 142, 164–66
Woodward, William E., 53
Woolf, Virginia, 123, 147, 176
Worbs, Frank, 62
Wordsworth, William, 130
Wright, Richard, 34
Wright, Sylvia, 115
Wylie, Philip, 115

Y
Yakumo, Koizumi (Lafcadio Hearn), 169

Z
Zangwill, Israel, 109–10
Zimmer, Ben, 134–35

A Note on the Author

PAUL DICKSON has written more than a dozen word books and dictionaries, including *Words from the White House*, *The Dickson Baseball Dictionary*, *The Congress Dictionary* (with Paul Clancy), *Family Words*, and *Slang*. He was a contributing editor with Merriam-Webster in charge of the Lighter Side of Language series, did a bylined commentary on language for NPR's *All Things Considered* in the 1990s, and was an occasional contributor to William Safire's "On Language" column in the *New York Times*. Dickson has coined two words of his own: *word word* (the lexical double construction heard in the question, "Are we talking about an e-book or a book book?") and *demonym* (the name for a person from a specific locality, e.g., New Yorker or Hoosier). He is also the author of the seminal narrative history *Sputnik: The Shock of the Century* and the coauthor of the acclaimed *The Bonus Army: An American Epic*. He lives in Garrett Park, Maryland.